ABOUT WHAT I KNOW

ZEN AND CONTEMPORARY KNOWLEDGE

A COMMENTARY TREATISE IN

QUESTION AND ANSWER FORMAT

THÍCH THÔNG TRIỆT

Buddhist calendar year: 2563 – Calendar Year: 2019

SUNYATA FOUNDATION
Perris, California

Copyright © 2014 by Thich Thong Triet (Vietnamese original)
Copyright © 2019 by Thich Thong Triet (English translation)

Materials contained in this book may be reproduced without permission from the publisher provided that you charge no fees of any kind. Otherwise, all rights reserved.

Translated from the Vietnamese by Sunyata Meditation students
Cover design by Tuệ Nguyên

First edition published 2019

Printed in the United States of America

ISBN 978-0-9986920-3-6 (paper)

Published by Sunyata Foundation
18525 Frantz Road
Perris, California 92570
www.sunyatameditation.org

Library of Congress Control Number: 2019901617

Contents

Contents i
Dedication iii
Acknowledgements v
Preface ix

INTRODUCTION 1

COMMENTARY TREATISE 1: INTRODUCING THE COMMENTARY FORMAT 9

COMMENTARY TREATISE 2: MY AIM IN DEVELOPING THESE COMMENTARIES 15
Why I have chosen the topic 16
Further Reading 1: The Bāhiya Sutta 34

COMMENTARY TREATISE 3: SIGNIFICANCE OF THE SUBJECT OF THIS BOOK 43
Significance of the Subject of Zen and Contemporary Knowledge 44
Further Reading 2: Tangible Benefits of Contemporary Knowledge 62

COMMENTARY TREATISE 4: A SPIRITUAL SCIENCE 77

COMMENTARY TREATISE 5: A NEW CONCEPT OF ZEN PRACTICE 125

COMMENTARY TREATISE 6: FOUR RELAY STATIONS IN THE HUMAN BRAIN 143
First Relay Station: Reticular Formation 144
Second Relay Station: Thalamus 154
Third Relay Station: Hypothalamus 157
Fourth Relay Station: Precuneus 164

COMMENTARY TREATISE 7: THERAPEUTIC EFFECTS OF ZEN ON PSYCHOLOGICAL AND PSYCHOSOMATIC ILLNESSES 171

Therapeutic Effects of Zen on Psychological and Psychosomatic Illnesses 172
Further Reading 3: Stress 180
Further Reading 4: Psychosomatic Illnesses 200

COMMENTARY TREATISE 8: RESULTS OF EXPERIMENTS PERFORMED ON MASTER REVEREND THÍCH THÔNG TRIỆT 211

COMMENTARY TREATISE 9: A DREAM BECAME REALITY 231

Ms. Minh Tuyền's Address at the Paris' Launch of Master's Book in June 2008 232
Brain Imaging Program in Stuttgart 238
A New Horizon 251

POSTFACE 271

Dedication

This book is dedicated to all meditation students who have attended the Śūnyatā Meditation courses in and outside the United States of America:

1. **USA:** *Southern California, San Jose, Sacramento (California); Florida; Houston (Texas); Portland (Oregon); Seattle (Washington State); Virginia; Washington D.C.; Michigan;*

2. **France:** *Paris, Toulouse;*

3. **Germany:** *Stuttgart, Frankfurt, Krefeld, Berlin;*

4. **Canada:** *Toronto, Ottawa, Montreal;*

5. **Switzerland:** *Lausanne;*

6. **Australia:** *Sydney, Adelaide, Melbourne, Cairns, Brisbane, Perth.*

Acknowledgements

For the Vietnamese original version

I would like to thank all the scientists who have contributed in the creation of the Functional Magnetic Resonance Imaging (f-MRI) machine and the Organization for Human Brain Mapping (OHBM) which has provided the opportunity for neuroscientists around the world to showcase their discoveries each year.

I would like to thank Professor Dr. Klaus Scheffler of the Department of Biomedical Magnetic Resonance, Tübingen University Hospital, Tübingen, Germany, for providing me the opportunity, time and equipment to perform this study.

I would like to thank Dr. Michael Erb, Dr. Ranganatha Sitaram, Mr. Ashish Kaul Sahib, Mr. Bankim Chander and other staff at the Department of Neuroradiology, Tübingen University Hospital, Tübingen, Germany involved in the brain imaging and electroencephalography (EEG) measurements for helping us - the Sunyata Meditation Association USA and the Sunyata Meditation Association Stuttgart - complete this program of brain imaging for members of the Sunyata Sangha and meditation students from 2007 to 2013. You have made a great contribution to Eastern experimental spiritual science as well as Western psychological and social sciences.

I would like to thank Dr. Phạm Văn Phú and Dr. Phạm Ngọc Thịnh, both meditation students of the Stuttgart Sunyata Meditation practice community, who created the favorable causal conditions that led to this study.

I would like to thank Mr. Quang Chiếu Nguyễn Văn Hùng, former president of the Sunyata Meditation Association

Stuttgart and the Stuttgart Sunyata Meditation practice community, who acted as liaison between me and the University of Tübingen in these past years.

I would like to thank Ms. Minh Huệ, head of the study team of the Stuttgart Sunyata Meditation practice community, who helped me liaise with Dr. Michael Erb in the last year.

I would like to acknowledge the following Sunyata meditation students who have contributed their effort and supporting causal conditions in the following activities:

- Bhikkhuni Zen Master Triệt Như for proof reading and reviewing the final document before printing.

- Mr. Tuệ Đạt for liaising with the translation teams of various practice communities and for typing the manuscript.

- Mr. Tuệ Nguyên for designing the book cover and organizing photos.

- Ms. Triệt Huệ, Mr. Không Giới and Ms. Thuần Chánh Tín for printing and distribution.

- Bhikkhuni Phúc Trí, Bhikkhuni Hạnh Như, and Ms. Minh Ngộ for looking after the Sunyata Meditation Perris Monastery.

To all Buddhists and meditation students who have directly or indirectly provided encouragement and assistance, including help in regard to Buddhist suttas and commentaries and scientific publications, I would like to transfer the merits that you have garnered by supporting the dhamma. May all Buddhas from the ten directions, in their compassion, bestow unto you their blessing and protection.

Thích Thông Triệt
Riverside, California
Buddhist calendar year 2558 – Calendar year 2014

For the English version

I would like to express my thanks to the following meditation students who have contributed to this English version of the book:

- Mr. Như Lưu for performing the translation into English.

- Ms. Hoàng Liên and Mr. Thông Như for reviewing the translation work.

- Ms. Jenny Barnett and Bhikkhu Thích Không Triệt for editing the English text after translation.

- Mr. Tuệ Nguyên for the design of the book cover.

- Mr. Như Lưu for the layout of the book interior.

- Mr. Tuệ Nguyên for organizing the printing of the book.

- Mr. Như Lưu for the online publishing and distribution of the book.

Thích Thông Triệt
Riverside, California
Buddhist calendar year 2563 – Calendar year 2019

Preface

This book, "Zen and Contemporary Knowledge - A Commentary Treatise in Question and Answer Format", is a collection of articles that I developed to teach meditation students and help them practice in practice communities in the USA and elsewhere between 1995 and 2014. Now, due to the causal conditions created by the closing in June 2013 of the brain imaging study conducted on myself and the drafting of a summary of the study by Dr. Michael Erb, I wish to consolidate into nine Commentary Treatises and four Further Readings a number of articles and photographs, new and old, that I previously had in various forms.

In some cases, I have put together in one Commentary Treatise several teaching articles that were not initially written in the logical order of a single event. This can lead to a lack of unity in the Commentary Treatise and instances of repetition on the same topic. I seek the understanding of readers.

All topics in the Commentary Treatises on Zen and Contemporary Knowledge focus on four main points:

1) Providing answers to the questions that I had after I realized in the beginning of 1982 that I had been practicing meditation incorrectly.

(2) This realization led me to view Buddhist meditation as an experimental spiritual science. It is a science aimed at training the individual to control their brain cells and get them to develop a new habit - the habit of not having inner chatter in the mind. Once a person has managed to keep their inner chatter under control, they will progressively be able to exploit the innate special

capabilities of their brain. These will help them to: (1) transform their incorrect perspectives; (2) bring harmony to their body and mind, and develop their own spiritual wisdom; (3) become a good member of society, based on the foundation of a spirit of service to others.

(3) My third area of focus is to draw a new horizon to the practice of meditation, one that combines Western scientific knowledge with Eastern meditation teaching through the images of my brain while in meditation. I have often said: "The East can explain and execute, but is unable to point to scientific evidence. On the other hand, the West can explain and point to scientific evidence, but does not know how to execute." Now, I hope to fill the gap by being able to explain, execute and point to scientific evidence as well.

(4) Finally, after 20 years, my dream of being able to take images of my brain while in meditation has become a reality. This is a testimony of the combination of the factors of will, capability, assiduous practice, and completion of causal conditions. Not talking about the dream lies at the base of these four processes. This is the Absolutely Pure Ego that is often mentioned in the Prajña Pāramitā suttas. This is what the Buddha called the Immobile Mind or the Tathā-Mind in the Nikāya suttas.

The causal conditions that allow this book to be published are now completed.

INTRODUCTION

Why meditation is valuable to human life

Establishing a clear perspective on meditation

Meditation does not perform miracles. It does not possess supernatural capabilities that bring salvation to all beings and help them escape suffering and sorrow. It is a *tool* that, if used wisely, can become a good tool that can help us transform our mind, end our suffering, and attain enlightenment and liberation from birth and death.

Some people think, in regard to meditation, that they need to be taught a practice that will help them achieve a *sudden spiritual realization* and become a Buddha.

Others think that they only need to learn the method to *see their true nature* and become a Buddha. They then hold onto these views and practice meditation in order to see their true nature and achieve a sudden spiritual realization. However, despite practicing over many years, they still cannot achieve a sudden spiritual realization or see their true nature. For this reason, seeing one's true nature and sudden spiritual realization become two topics of meditation that are both *mysterious and attractive.*

We will never be able to *come face to face* with meditation if we approach meditation with these views. This is because sudden spiritual realization and seeing our true nature require us to follow a systematic process of learning and practice over a long period of time and do not occur haphazardly as some might have thought. Prince Siddhattha attained Buddhahood by progressing through four stages of meditation, and by following an orderly process. In the final stage of meditation, he attained the state called the "Tathā-Mind". This state is beyond words and is founded upon the "immobility of the three mental formation processes". In the book "The Buddha's Process of Spiritual Cultivation, Realization and Enlightenment - A Treatise and Commentaries in Question and Answer Format", I have explained in detail the meaning of "Immobility of the Three Mental Formation Processes" and identified the *true natures* that Prince Siddhattha *saw* when he became a Buddha.

In order to avoid any misconception about meditation, I always open my teaching classes with the topic "Why meditation is valuable to our life". My purpose is to clearly define our attitude when we start our meditation journey. We should approach meditation with humility, without excessive expectation, and without desire for things that are beyond our capability.

Marvelous capability

However, it is true that when meditation is practiced with the correct method, the correct technique and in accordance with the Wordless Awareness Mind or our faculty for self-awareness, it does indeed have marvelous capabilities. These are:

- It helps keep our body in harmonious balance, i.e. maintain an internal harmony between our internal organs, our circulatory system, our internal energy system, our muscular system, our skeletal system, our skin system. From a state of illness, meditation can help us alleviate or cure a number of common illnesses such as high blood pressure, cardio vascular illnesses, high cholesterol, asthma, allergies, or regulate the level of blood glucose.

- It helps rebalance our mind and cure a number of psychological illnesses such as chronic stress, depression, memory impairment, anxiety, clinging to things, pride, arrogance, believing in one's superiority. Buddhist terminology refers to the illnesses of clinging to the reality of the self, clinging to one's perspectives, clinging to the reality of objects. As we practice meditation, we become more understanding, tolerant, forgiving and sympathetic toward others. We naturally live with wisdom and compassion toward all beings.

- It helps maintain a harmonious balance between our body and mind. We will experience living in harmony with everyone around us, from our family to society, to the environment.

- At a higher level, meditation can help us develop our spiritual wisdom. We will develop the ability to find creative and innovative solutions to problems in our own sphere of specialty. Furthermore, we will develop the capacity for eloquence and the energy of loving-kindness, compassion, sympathetic joy and equanimity.

- Further still, meditation is able to guide us toward *experiencing being a witness*. With this ability, we will be able to be in control of our karmic consciousness when we leave this world. We will be able to prevent the unwholesome near-death karma from arising.

By practicing meditation regularly, we will be able to experience the afore-mentioned logical, practical and marvelous capabilities. There is nothing mysterious about this. The "miracle" of meditation resides simply in the processes of knowing, awareness and cognitive awareness.

Thus everyone can successfully practice meditation.

We do not develop illusory ideas when practicing meditation.

In summary, a human being consists of three elements: body, mind, and spiritual wisdom. We will recognize the practical value of meditation in our life when we practice meditation with the correct method, correct technique, and consistent with the functions of the brain that support the Wordless Awareness Mind and the Tathā-Mind.

The capabilities that I mentioned above are based on the principle of action and effect in spirituality.

The principle of action and effect

In the field of meditation, the action and effect principle is a practical principle. Action is what we do. Effect is the result or outcome of what we do. If we act correctly, we reap a favorable result. And if we act incorrectly, we reap an unfavorable result. This principle forms part of the topic of bio feedback in meditation. This means that any meditation practice will result in a beneficial or adverse result on our body, mind, and spiritual wisdom. Why? This is because our body is a living organism. In this organism, from our brain to our nervous system, endocrine system, internal organs and muscular system there are fluids with chemical compounds called biochemical substances. They are also called hormones. They have the ability to make our body healthy or ill, our mind peaceful or despondent, and our memory impaired or long lasting.

As I have practiced meditation for a long time, I have been able to experience this fact. Incorrect practice leads to illness while correct practice leads to good health. But what is a correct practice and what is an incorrect one?

We are practicing meditation correctly if we follow the teaching of the Buddha and Buddhist Patriarchs, we do not exert excessive effort, we do not try too hard, and we do not concentrate our mind on the object of meditation. We practice comfortably, *leisurely*, in a relaxed manner, but regularly. We do not miss a practice session in our daily routine, but we do not focus on exerting our will to *oppress the body, oppress the mind* and maintain a sitting position. The more we oppress body and mind, the more we suffer from illnesses such as high blood pressure, diabetes and obesity.

We practice meditation in the four postures – walking, standing, lying, and sitting (leisurely or in the formal posture) – using the techniques that the Buddha taught us at the fundamental level. We apply the following techniques: knowing, just knowing, knowing clearly and completely (called Full and Clear Awareness in the suttas), and knowing things as they are, in the four postures. These methods activate directly one of the three awareness faculties of the Wordless Awareness Mind. We do not meander along, we do not "use a rock to crush the grass", and we do not oppress the body and mind. This meditation practice will result in biochemical substances such as serotonin, melatonin, acetylcholine, endorphin, dopamine, and insulin, etc. being secreted from the parasympathetic nervous system, the hypothalamus, the endocrine system, and the brain stem.

We are practicing meditation incorrectly if we follow the teaching of the Buddha and Buddhist Patriarchs but exert too much effort, try too hard, and concentrate too much on the topics of meditation. Or we practice using the functions of the Consciousness, Thinking Faculty or distorted

Intellect*. This meditation practice will result in the sympathetic nervous system being continuously activated, which in turn results in the secretion of biochemical substances that are harmful to our body. Examples of these substances are: norepinephrine (or noradrenaline), epinephrine (or adrenaline), cortisol, and glucagon, etc.

Although meditation deals in spirituality, it is also an experimental science. When we practice meditation, all our brain cells and areas of the cerebral cortex, limbic system, memory areas, nervous system, and endocrine system are affected through two response mechanisms:

1. A "sensory response" that consists of an activation of the ultimate faculties of the Wordless Awareness Mind through the sensory organs.

2. An "intrinsically-generated response" that consists of an activation of the self-awareness faculty of the precuneus through cognitive awareness.

The sensory response leads to spiritual realization. The intrinsically-generated response leads to complete spiritual realization.

---

* Note for the English version: an ordinary person's mind (also called "worldly mind" or "false mind" in Buddhist texts) consists of three main functions. The Thinking Faculty is where thinking, pondering, reasoning and judging are generated based on memory and past experience; it is located in the left pre-frontal cortex and is referred to in Buddhist texts as the past-oriented mind. The Intellect is a special part of the Thinking Faculty that is involved in reasoning, speculation, deduction, and planning; it is referred to in Buddhist texts as the future-oriented mind. The Consciousness makes sense of reality by dualistic differentiation and includes the need to report and act; it is located in the right pre-frontal cortex, and is referred to in Buddhist texts as the present-oriented mind.

I have expounded these principles since the end of 1997 when I started to teach meditation students to aim directly at the Wordless Awareness Mind.

I hope that you understand clearly the action and effect principle that governs meditation, and that you avoid the pitfalls of an incorrect meditation practice.

COMMENTARY TREATISE 1: INTRODUCING THE COMMENTARY FORMAT

Introducing the Commentary Format

Hypothetical dialogue

To begin the process of developing my commentary and question-answers, I conceive a hypothetical situation where a person asks me questions about a meditation practice topic. This leads me to provide answers, or ask questions back to ascertain whether the person understands the matter. Thus I create a format of question and answer around a topic, with the aim of bringing clarity to it.

In every topic covered in the commentary treatises, I always begin by defining the idioms and specialized terminology that pertain to this topic. I see this definition section as setting the direction and destination for the practitioner. This part is very important to people new to the practice of meditation. If they misconstrue the idioms and specialized terminology used in the meditation texts, they may practice incorrectly and suffer serious consequences to their body, mind, and spiritual wisdom.

In order to provide a clear and complete answer to the question, I often raise a number of secondary questions to provide more perspective around the main topic. This is a way to enrich the topic so that it becomes clearer and more complete. My aim is to help the practitioner establish a correct direction and use the correct means in their journey. If this objective is achieved, the questions and answers will benefit those who have just commenced their journey in meditation, or those who have practiced for a long time without making progress.

Action and effect

The most important point in the practice of meditation is its effect on the body, mind, and spiritual wisdom of the practitioner. This effect is the result of the techniques and practices that the practitioner uses when applying the teaching of the Buddha and Buddhist Patriarchs.

For this reason, you need to understand clearly the principle of action and effect in regard to the practice of meditation and its effects on:

- the cerebral cortex,
- the limbic system,
- the autonomic nervous system,
- the endocrine system,

and in turn their effects on the internal organs. If you do not understand clearly the principle of action and effect when you practice meditation, you may bring about detrimental effects on your body, mind, and spiritual wisdom. For example, your body may change from a state of health to illness; your mind may change from a state of detachment to attachment; your spiritual wisdom may change from a state of clarity to ignorance, clinging to the reality of self, clinging to one's own perspective, and clinging to the reality of objects. This then leads to multiple forms of struggle, perversion, and endless dispute and conflict in your everyday life. The end result is the loss of all the noble objectives of meditation, which are a changed perspective in life, freedom from suffering, enlightenment, and liberation from birth and death.

The question-and-answer section is thus highly important. I endeavor to use many forms and contents in the questions and answers to bring more clarity to the topic. When I think that the topic has been sufficiently covered, I move on to another topic through another question.

Back and forth questioning and answering

I usually start a question and answer section with a brief commentary and then explain the meaning of this commentary with a set of back and forth questions and answers. My aims in developing these back and forth questions and answers are two-fold:

1. First, to answer any questions that the meditation practitioner may have in regard to idioms and specialized terminology used in meditation texts and thus help the practitioner avoid any misunderstanding.

2. Second, to help the meditation practitioner realize through these back and forth questions and answers the important aspects of the topic. The meditation practitioner will then be able to practice in accordance with the "biofeedback principle in meditation".

Example 1

Let us assume that a person wishes to have an answer to a question about their past practice of meditation. They ask:

Question: Master, could you please explain the principle of action and effect in meditation?

Answer: The principle of action and effect in meditation is the principle that underlies the mutual interaction between:

- The mind.

INTRODUCING THE COMMENTARY FORMAT 13

- The Buddhist teaching.

- The brain, consisting of the pre-frontal cortex in the left and right hemispheres, and the area at the back of the left hemisphere.

- The limbic system, consisting of the thalamus, the hypothalamus, endocrine glands, and memory areas: short term memory, emotional memory (the amygdala), and long term memory.

- The cranial nervous system and the spinal nervous system.

- The autonomic nervous system consisting of the sympathetic nervous system and the parasympathetic nervous system.

- The endocrine system.

This mutual interaction results in the secretion of biochemical substances at the extremities of the sympathetic nervous system or parasympathetic nervous system, or inside the endocrine glands. These substances lead to beneficial or detrimental effects on the body, mind, and spiritual wisdom of the meditation practitioner depending on the technique and practice they use.

Question: Master, could you please explain the meaning of the term "mind" that you just mentioned? Could you clarify what mind, among the types of mind mentioned in Buddhism, is referred to in this context?

Answer: The mind referred to in this context is the True Mind, or Wordless Awareness Mind.

Question: Master, could you please explain the meaning of the term "self" in this context, what is it really?

Answer: The self in this context refers to the "Pure and Tranquil Self" or the "Pure and Tranquil Ego".

Question: Master, how do we know the purity and tranquility characters of this self?

Answer: All you need to do is stop the verbal chatter in your mind. At that very moment, you immediately experience the purity and tranquility of your mind.

Question: Master, could you please explain why stopping the verbal chatter in the mind is equivalent to the Buddhist term "Pure and Tranquil"?

Answer: The reason is that, when you stop the verbal chatter in your mind, you continue to be aware through seeing, hearing, and touch. This knowing-by-seeing, knowing-by-hearing, and knowing-by-touch is what is known in Buddhist terminology as the "Pure and Tranquil Ego" or the "Pure and Tranquil Self".

Question: Thank you, Master! This is the first time that we have heard this explanation that the Buddhist term "Pure and Tranquil" has the same meaning as "Not having verbal chatter in the mind". And, Master, what faculty is represented by the Buddhist term "Absolutely Pure and Tranquil Ego"?

Answer: This is the Tathā-Mind's role.

COMMENTARY TREATISE 2:

MY AIM IN DEVELOPING

THESE COMMENTARIES

Why I have chosen the topic "Commentary Treatise on Zen and Contemporary Knowledge"

First reason

- **Marking a new era where Eastern meditation is bringing new light to Western scientists**

After my *spiritual realization* that occurred in 1982 while I was in prison, I continually experienced a sense of joy arising in my mind and no longer worried about recovering my freedom. I accepted that it was a karmic debt that I needed to repay. When this karmic debt ends, I will be set free. As long as it has not ended, I will just stay here to repay it!

Then, one day, I suddenly heard from the prison cadre that I was to be transferred to another prison camp. The prison cadre took me to another area within the Thanh Liệt prison camp to wait for the transport to the Hà Tây concentration camp. When I arrived there, I saw several fellow prisoners with hollow faces and emaciated bodies. I knew some of them previously, but at that time, I could not recognize any. The prison cadre pointed at me and said:

- Of all of you here, you have been inside the longest. How is it that you have such a radiant and rosy face?

When I heard this comment, I thought a word of encouragement to myself: you have been practicing correctly! But I didn't know at the time in what way my practice was correct. I only remembered a comment by a fellow prisoner when I was at the B-5 prison camp in Long

Thành. One day, when we were doing our morning toilet, he asked me: "Venerable monk, you look quite young still, are you 80 yet?" I forced a smile and responded: "No, not yet!" At the time, I was just over 40 and had been in prison for only two years...

Now, five years later, here was the prison cadre complimenting me on looking young and rosy-faced. This told me that I had been practicing correctly.

When I arrived at the Hà Tây concentration camp, I met some old friends and obtained a mirror to check how I looked. I saw that my face indeed reflected an inner radiance. Several old friends paid me a visit and commented: "Now I know that you are practicing correctly!" This led me to ask myself the question: "How does this correct practice come about?" My body, that had previously aged prematurely, had become young and healthy looking in just five years.

I then started to surmise that the correctness of my meditation practice must have had some effect on my brain. There must be some substances that are secreted inside the brain and that make me healthy, joyful and glowing with inner radiance. Similarly, when I practiced incorrectly, there must also have been some chemical substances that were secreted and caused premature aging.

From that point on, I developed the wish to study the science of neurology when I recovered my freedom, in order to understand what happens in the brain when one has a spiritual realization, and what chemical substances are secreted in the brain when one's meditation practice runs into an impasse.

I was then transferred to the Hà Tây prison camp in North Vietnam. In March 1985, I was transferred alone to the south of Vietnam and continued my *unsolicited retreat* at a special prison on Trần Bình Trọng Street, in the 5th district of Saigon. In September 1986, I was transferred to the Chí Hòa prison and in February 1989, I was set free.

I returned to the Thường Chiếu monastery, and met my Master, Venerable Thích Thanh Từ, during the Tết festivities. Master and student were filled with mixed feelings of joy and sorrow... I presented to my Master what I had realized in my 14 years of prison.

During this meeting, I presented my vow to my Master: "If causal conditions are met, I will present the teaching of my Master in a form that reconciles with the scientific knowledge of the brain. I saw my body looking like the body of an 80-year old, with many illnesses, emaciated and especially lacking inner radiance. Then I saw this same body becoming younger and glowing with inner radiance. I think there is something in action inside a person's brain that leads to the transformation of their body and mind". My Master agreed.

At the beginning of 1991, my Master published a book on meditation entitled "Vietnamese Zen Buddhism at the End of the Twentieth Century". He gave me a copy and asked for my comments. After I completed reading the book, I came back to Thường Chiếu and presented to my Master this opinion: "Please give me permission to explain your teaching using explanatory diagrams and scientific explanations". My Master agreed. It was thus that I stayed in the private quarters of Venerable Nhật Quang, resident abbot of Thường Chiếu, to develop an explanation of my Master's teaching on meditation using drawings of the

AIM OF THESE COMMENTARIES 19

brain. On October 10th, 1992, I completed the book "Explaining Zen using Diagrams".

At the end of 1992 (on November 24th, 1992), before my departure for resettlement in the USA, my Master convened a meeting in his private quarters at the Thường Chiếu monastery. My Master's main objective for the meeting was to *officialize,* in front of the congregation of monks at Thường Chiếu, my explanation of his teaching using neurological science through my book "Explaining Zen using Diagrams". He gave the following validation:

"This collection of Explanatory Diagrams that Thông Triệt has developed to explain the meditation method that I teach in my book "Vietnamese Zen Buddhism at the End of the Twentieth Century" can be considered a Buddhist commentary. Like all Buddhist commentaries, it needs to accord with the thinking and perspectives of our time. Our time is the time of experimental science. This is why the language and diagrams that Thông Triệt *tentatively uses* to explain and support my teaching also need to accord with our contemporary thinking so that they are better received by educated people. This is a logical thing."

I arrived in the USA at the end of 1992 but it wasn't until 1995 that I realized my wish to publish the series "Explaining Zen using Diagrams" consisting of two books.

This was the first step that I took to bring Vietnamese Zen Buddhism into the Western scientific sphere.

Second reason

- **My dream of taking brain images to identify the areas of the brain that relate to the teaching of the Buddha**

When I arrived in the USA at the end of 1992, I first settled in Seattle, Washington. In the middle of 1993, I travelled to Hawaii to visit a friend. Through an extraordinary causal condition, the person who met me at the airport was Ms. Helene Phan-Thanh together with her husband, Dr. David Johnson, a professor in Psychology at the University of Hawaii. I used the word "extraordinary causal condition" because when Ms. Helene Phan-Thanh greeted me at the airport, instead of the usual greetings, she handed me a copy of the Zen explanatory diagrams in large format that I recently completed in Vietnam and presented to my Master before I departed for the USA. I was very surprised to see this set of drawings. I subsequently became a friend of the Johnson family.

During my stay in Hawaii, Dr. Johnson took me on a visit to the University of Hawaii. While there, I saw an 800-page book about the remarkable functions of the hypothalamus. I asked Dr. Johnson to borrow the book for me.

When I bid farewell to the Johnsons to return to the US mainland, I received another gift. They promised to donate to me a house in Oregon so that I could have a settled place to live.

This house was the very place where I later welcomed my Master in October, 1994. My Master officially recognized this location in Oregon as the first established Sunyata Meditation House. Following that, I started at this location, on January 1st, 1995, the first Sunyata Fundamental Meditation Course.

Early on, when I was in Seattle (in 1993), I had the opportunity to read an issue of the *Scientific American* magazine publishing images taken by neurologists using a PET (Positron Emission Tomography) machine of four

AIM OF THESE COMMENTARIES 21

areas of the brain: (1) the seeing area, (2) the hearing area, (3) the concept decoding area or Broca area, and (4) the inner speech area that lies next to the motor cortex. When I read this article, I dreamt that I would one day have the opportunity to take images of two more areas, the touch area and the cognitive awareness area, in order to completely locate the four ultimate faculties that the Buddha mentioned in the Bāhiya sutta.

In mid-1994, when Dr. Johnson travelled to Seattle to take me to Oregon and complete the property transfer process, I asked him whether he could help me liaise with the Scientific American magazine and ask them to take images of my brain. He told me that this was a very difficult undertaking due to the costs involved. Furthermore, at the time, science had not identified the existence of the touch area and cognitive awareness area.

I was not discouraged and continued to hold the hope and confidence that one day I would be able to fulfill this dream, I knew that I had to develop the ability to enter samādhi as easily as *clicking my fingers.*

Silently holding the hope

I then no longer thought about this matter, and instead applied myself to practicing samādhi meditation by continually raising the No Talk thought until it held steady in the four postures: walking, standing, lying, and sitting. When I wanted to raise a thought it would happen, otherwise thoughts would remain still in the knowing area of the Wordless Awareness Mind or in the cognitive awareness area of Buddha-nature (or the Tathā-Mind). Only then could the dream of taking brain images become a reality.

It was 12 years later that causal conditions were completely present. In 2006, when I was on a teaching trip to Germany, my dream of taking brain images started to become a reality. I had help from a young couple who were both doctors, Dr. Phạm Ngọc Thịnh and Dr. Pham Văn Phú, who had patiently and persistently *knocked* on the door of many organizations specializing in brain imaging, but without success. Finally, when causal conditions were completely present, Dr. Thịnh *knocked* on the right door and the *door* immediately opened.

Dr. Thịnh managed to contact Dr. Michael Erb who agreed to start in April 2006 an experimental program using the f-MRI equipment with two meditation students from the Stuttgart practice community, Ms. Minh Vân and Mr. Quang Nguyên. Following that, in June 2007, the program to take brain images of myself and members of the Sunyata Sangha officially commenced.

The following years (in 2008, 2009, 2010) I alone was involved in the brain imaging experiments. Finally, I was able to fulfill my dream of proving the existence and location of the four ultimate faculties that the Buddha mentioned to Bāhiya in the Bāhiya sutta (*refer to Further Reading 1 on the Bāhiya sutta*).

These four ultimate faculties are: Ultimate Seeing, Ultimate Hearing, Ultimate Touch, and Ultimate Cognitive Awareness. In particular, we could also point to the areas related to Inner Talk and Inner Dialogue in the frontal lobe area.

At the beginning of 2010, Dr. Erb took images of my brain while I was practicing the four samādhi meditation stages:

- Samādhi with Inner Talk and Inner Dialogue.

- Samādhi without Inner Talk and Inner Dialogue.
- Full and Clear Awareness Samādhi.
- Suchness-Samādhi, also called Immobility Samādhi (Akuppā Samādhi).

Following the successful completion of the experimental program, Dr. Michael Erb and Dr. Ranganatha Sitaram published the results at the 16th Annual Meeting of the Organization of Human Brain Mapping (OHBM) that took place from June 6th to June 10th, 2010 in Barcelona, Spain. The following year, in June 2011, the results were again displayed at the 17th Annual Meeting of the OHBM, in Québec City, Canada.

At this point, I considered that my dream of "taking brain images to identify the brain areas that correspond to the teaching of the Buddha" had become a reality.

Third reason:

- **The time has come ...**

I considered that the time had arrived for me to publish the images of my brain that show the areas that correspond to functions mentioned by the Buddha in his discourses, such as False Thoughts and the False Mind, and how these processes occur within the human brain. One of the most interesting outcomes occurred in 2008 when I practiced the "Bare Attention" meditation technique while my arm was being scratched by a brush in order to identify where Ultimate Touch is located.

24 AIM OF THESE COMMENTARIES

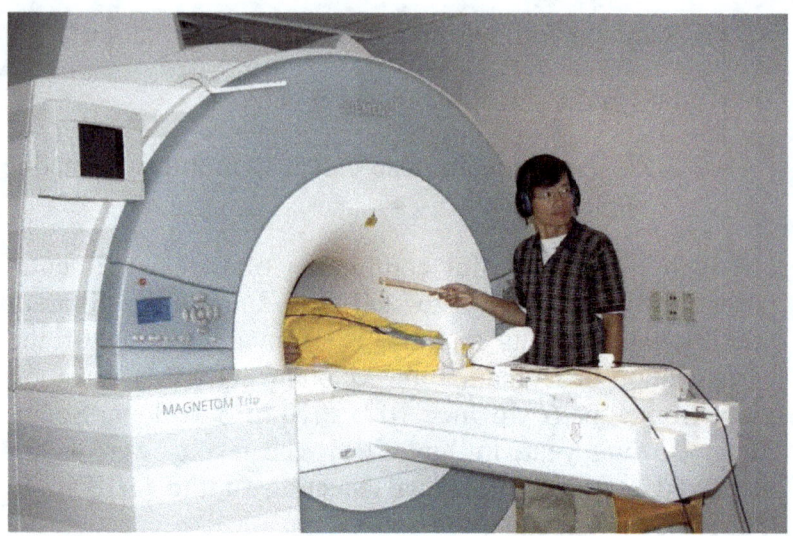

I expected to see an area that corresponded to Ultimate Touch, but the surprising outcome was that all four ultimate faculties appeared, namely:

1. Ultimate Touch
2. Ultimate Hearing
3. Ultimate Seeing
4. Ultimate Cognitive Awareness

AIM OF THESE COMMENTARIES

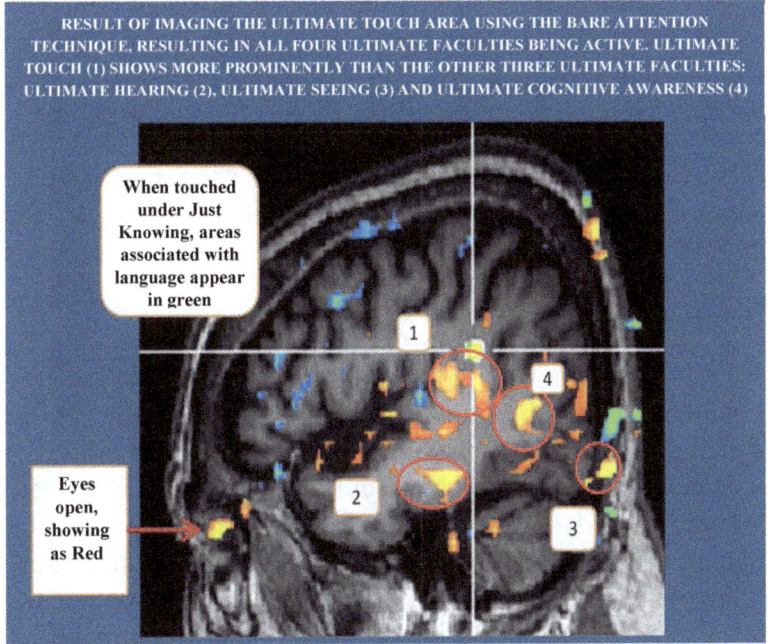

Causal conditions leading to my participation in the OHBM Annual Meeting in June 2010 in Barcelona

In December 2009, I asked Mr. Quang Chiếu, a meditation student of the Stuttgart Sunyata practice community, to contact Dr. Erb and ask whether he would agree to conduct the brain imaging exercise at the beginning of 2010 instead of June 2010 as previously planned. Dr. Erb agreed. At 8 am on January 3rd, 2010, I arrived at the brain imaging facility together with Mr. Quang Chiếu, Mr. Tuệ Giác and Ms. Triệt Huệ. This turned out to be the longest brain imaging session. At 3 pm, Dr. Erb asked us to come into his office and commented that this batch of brain images were excellent. He then asked me: "Would you allow us to take the images of your brain to the Annual Meeting of the

OHBM that takes place in Barcelona in June this year?" When I heard this surprising question, some spiritual insights immediately occurred to me. I answered calmly, as if I was expecting such a request. I nodded and said: "Yes, I want to!"

This was why in June of that year, for the first time, a "peasant monk" attended the Annual Meeting of the OHBM, at its 16th Session in Barcelona, Spain.

Returning to the past

In my years teaching meditation students from the Fundamental Meditation Course to the Wisdom Level Meditation Courses, I have drawn diagrams to show the working of the four ultimate faculties of the brain: Ultimate Seeing located in the occipital lobe, Ultimate Hearing located in the temporal lobe, Ultimate Touch located in the the parietal lobe, and Ultimate Cognitive Awareness located in the parietal lobe at the center of the other three faculties. In one of my classes, there was a female student who asked me: "Master, are you sure that this is the location of the Ultimate Cognitive Awareness faculty? Today, we need to be "evidence based". If you teach something, you need to provide trustworthy evidence. If you just draw a diagram like this, who would believe you?" Furthermore, when I described the Buddhist term *Force of Wisdom*, I always drew a straight line representing the exterior of the cerebral cortex, and underneath it I drew several arrows representing the arising of the Force of Wisdom. What I wanted to represent was that the Force of Wisdom resides at the bottom of the Ultimate Cognitive Awareness faculty. When we stimulate the Ultimate Cognitive Awareness faculty through our practice, the Force of Wisdom gradually develops. At this point of my discourse, a student who was

AIM OF THESE COMMENTARIES

also a medical doctor said: "Master, some of us here are educated people, how can we believe what you are teaching?" Another student, who was also a medical doctor, told the first one: "My friend, don't embarrass Master. It is impossible for Master to prove this. Just listen to the teaching and get the meaning of it". I heard the comment and said immediately: "Thank you, Doctor, for raising this point. I have a book launch soon in San Jose, please attend as I will present the evidence that I have been quietly gathering over the last few years with Dr. Michael Erb at the University of Tübingen."

At the launch of the book "Zen in the Light of Science" in early 2008, I proclaimed the role of the precuneus, located in the parietal lobe of the cerebral cortex, as the source of the *force of wisdom*.

> **THE BUDDHA-MIND AREA (PRECUNEUS) APPEARS INSIDE THE BRAIN IN THE PARIETAL LOBE WHEN MASTER APPLIED THE TECHNIQUE OF AWAKE AWARENESS**

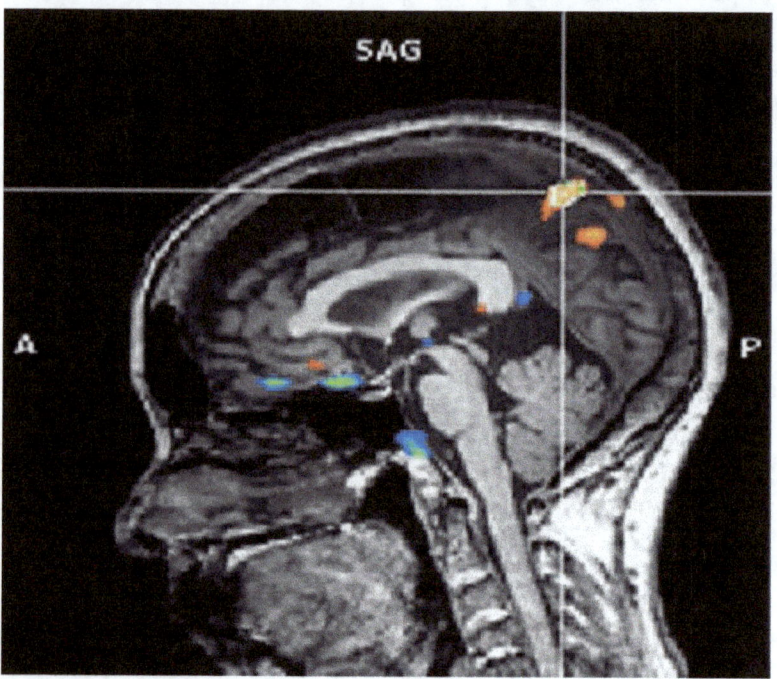

Fourth reason:

- Using neuroscience to show the exact processes through which meditation affects our body, mind and spiritual wisdom when we practice using the correct method. Conversely, how an incorrect meditation method affects our body, mind, and spiritual wisdom.

Question: What is practicing using the correct method? What are the outcomes?

Answer: The correct method, whatever the technique we adopt in our practice, uses our wordless awareness faculty. When we use the correct method, signals are sent to the hypothalamus that triggers the parasympathetic nervous system into secreting the biochemical acetylcholine. This in turn has a cascading effect on our endocrine system and our internal organs. As a result, our body is in harmonious balance, our mind is in harmonious balance, and our spiritual wisdom progressively develops.

Question: And what is practicing using an incorrect method? What are the outcomes?

Answer: We are following an incorrect method if we exert effort, concentrate or focus our attention on an object, or use our imagination, or use auto-suggestion. When we do so, we exercise our verbal knowing, which is located in our pre-frontal cortex. Signals are raised that activate the sympathetic nervous system. It secretes at its extremities the biochemical norepinephrine, resulting in psychosomatic illnesses and an agitated mind. This form of knowing is just worldly knowledge.

Fifth reason:

- **Using scientific knowledge to support the teaching of the Buddha that has remained valid after more than 25 centuries. This reason is especially applicable to those countries that are advanced in science and technology.**

Question: Could you please elaborate further?

Answer: If we want our message to be more easily accepted by a scientifically-minded audience, we need to provide clear explanations and tangible evidence using images and modern equipment.

Question: Master, could you please give concrete examples of teachings of the Buddha that have remained valid?

Answer: I would like to give as examples the truths that the Buddha discovered when he became enlightened, such as the Law of Co-dependent Arising and the Law of Dependently Arisen Phenomena. Through this teaching, the Buddha presented an order that governs the evolution of all worldly phenomena. They interact with each other to come into being and to cease to exist, and are not governed by the organizing and arranging hand of a deity or creator. Furthermore, the Buddha realized three characteristics of all worldly phenomena that remain valid nowadays. They are: impermanence, suffering or conflict, and insubstantiality.

Question: Master, could you please explain the meaning of enlightenment?

Answer: Enlightenment is a spiritual insight that originates from the Tathā-Mind, which is also our Buddha-nature, operating in the precuneus. This insight is novel in nature and has not been proclaimed by anyone. It is not an insight that originates from the Thinking Faculty, the Consciousness or the Intellect. Neither is it an insight that comes from the three ultimate faculties of the Wordless Awareness Mind: Ultimate Seeing, Ultimate Hearing and Ultimate Touch. For this reason, what are realized through enlightenment are truths that are eternally valid, regardless of time and place.

Question: Master, can we say that Buddhism is a philosophy?

AIM OF THESE COMMENTARIES 31

Answer: The Law of Co-Dependent Arising and the Law of Dependently Arisen Phenomena that the Buddha realized have frequently been called philosophies. Several Buddhist commentators have adopted a philosophical perspective and consider the Law of Co-Dependent Arising - Law of Dependently Arisen Phenomena a philosophy. A half-century ago, Mr. Hu Shih, a renowned Chinese Buddhist scholar living in the era of the Chiang Kai-shek regime, had a debate with Dr. Suzuki, a Japanese Zen Buddhism scholar living in England, on the topic: "Is the Law of Co-dependent Arising - Law of Dependently Arisen Phenomena a philosophy?" Mr. Hu Shih argued for the affirmative while Dr. Suzuki contended that what the Buddha saw in enlightenment cannot be considered a philosophy.

Philosophies are in reality based on discursive thinking, which originates from the Thinking Faculty, Consciousness and Intellect. For this reason, philosophies are only valid within a limited time period and limited geographical area, and are not everlasting. For example, the views of philosophers such as Socrates, Plato, Confucius, or Karl Marx are only valid within a certain time period because they are the product of the self. On the other hand, the Buddha's enlightenment occurred through the process of a sudden and intrinsically generated response that originated from his Buddha-nature (or the precuneus area). There was no thinking, reasoning, and discrimination involved.

In summary, these were the five reasons that led to my development of these Commentaries.

I hope that this "Zen and Contemporary Knowledge – A Commentary Treatise in Question and Answer Format" book will be of some help to those who wish to understand

Zen and want to practice it to experience its transformative effects on their mind and character, the harmonious balance between their body and mind, and the development of their spiritual wisdom.

Introduction to the Further Reading articles

In addition to the main teaching articles, I have developed support teaching articles for the purpose of helping meditation students gain a better understanding of Zen theory, Buddhist theory, meditation practice techniques, and science topics relevant to the practice of meditation. These Further Readings cover many topics, including an explanation of specialized terminology pertaining to Zen theory, Buddhist theory, meditation practice techniques, and science topics that aim to complement the materials covered in the main teaching articles. You may wish to read these Further Readings in your spare time as they may increase your knowledge of Zen theory and provide supporting causal conditions to your silent practice whenever you find the opportunity to practice.

Under the principle of action and response, Zen theory, Buddhist theory, meditation practice techniques, and scientific understanding are four means of learning that are necessary for beginners or mid-level students of meditation. I consider them to be practical and modern accessories for the spiritual traveller at the threshold of this 21st century.

I hope that these Further Readings will help those who have just committed themselves to the path of meditation to understand the essence and focus of the method of studying and practicing meditation in accordance with the principle of action and response. They will gain a higher confidence on their own path to "silently return home" without fear of losing their way.

Further Reading 1: The Bāhiya Sutta

The Bāhiya Sutta records the teaching of the Buddha on the faculties that constitute the Wordless Awareness Mind: Ultimate Seeing, Ultimate Hearing, Ultimate Touch, and Ultimate Cognitive Awareness. This sutta is part of the first chapter entitled Bodhi Vagga (Enlightenment Chapter) of the Udāna (The Exalted Unprompted Discourses). The Udāna are part of the Khuddaka Nikāya (the Minor Discourses of the Buddha) which are themselves part of the Discourses Basket (sutta piṭaka) of the Pāli texts of Early Buddhism.

The sutta recounts the case of instantaneous and complete spiritual realization attained by Bāhiya when he listened to a discourse of the Buddha. A precondition was that Bāhiya had a great question on how to attain everlasting happiness and peace. Upon hearing the teaching of the Buddha, he immediately and completely realized the truth and attained the state of Arahat.

A brief biography of Bāhiya

Bāhiya was an Arahat of the time of Gotama Buddha. He was known by this name for he lived in the village of Bāhiya in Bhārukaccha. People also called him Dārucīriya for he used to wear tree bark as clothing before he attained the state of Arahat. Dāru = tree; cīriya = bark; Dārucīriya: the one who wears bark clothing.

Before he pursued the spiritual path, he was a trader who plied his trade by boat. Seven times he sailed down the Indus and crossed the sea to trade. He was successful on all seven occasions. On the eighth trip, when he was on his way to the port of Suvaṇṇabhūmi, his boat capsized while he was at sea. His cargo, gold, and belongings sank to the bottom of the sea. All the traders on the boat perished but, fortunately for him, he managed to cling to a wooden plank. After seven days drifting at sea and fighting death, he washed up on the shore of Suppāraka with his plank. When he reached the shore, he did not have any clothing to hide his body, so he gathered small twigs and tree bark to make a loin cloth for himself. He then ventured further inland to beg for food. The villagers in the Suppāraka area saw his loin cloth made from tree bark and called him "the one who wears bark clothing" (Dārucīriya). They understood his predicament of being a shipwreck survivor, and each of them respectfully donated food to him according to their means. They saw that he did not have any clothing and wanted to donate to him clothing and other valuable items, but he refused and only accepted just what he needed. As a result, his prestige among the villagers increased. They soon believed that he was an Arahat. Eventually he himself thought that he was an Arahat or someone who had entered the path to Arahat-hood.

One night, a heavenly being (devatā) who was in the past a relative of Bāhiya appeared to him and informed him that he was not an Arahat, nor had he entered the path to Arahat-hood. If he wished to pursue the path to become an Arahat, he should without delay go to the Jetavana monastery in Sāvatthi and seek the Buddha. The Buddha would teach him the path to becoming an Arahat and how to reap the benefits of the spiritual path.

On hearing this, Bāhiya resolved to go immediately to Sāvatthi. With his strong determination, he covered the distance between Suppāraka and Sāvatthi in one night, despite it being 120 leagues or 480 km (a league or *yojana* is 4-km long). He hoped to meet the Buddha and hear directly the teaching on how to attain long lasting happiness and bliss.

At dawn on the following day, he arrived at the Jetavana monastery. He was filled with joy as he believed he would be able to meet the Buddha and greet him. But he was told that the Buddha had gone on his alms round. Filled with eagerness, he hurried in the direction that the Buddha had taken. He hoped that when he met the Buddha, he would be taught the practice method. He saw the Buddha walking at a gentle pace, hurried to place himself in front of the Buddha, knelt down in the middle of the road, prostrated himself at the feet of the Buddha to pay his respects, and collectedly solicited the Buddha to teach him the method to attain liberation.

He clasped his hands and said with all sincerity:

- O Blessed One, I pray that you would bestow your teaching upon me. O Gone-to-Goodness One, please teach me the way to long lasting happiness and bliss.

The Buddha gently responded:

- This is not the time, O Bāhiya, I am on my alms round.

Bāhiya reiterated his plea:

- O Blessed One! It is difficult to predict the obstacles that may affect your life, or may affect my life. O Blessed One, please teach me the way. O Gone-to-Goodness One, please teach me the way, which may help me attain long lasting happiness and bliss.

The Buddha declined a second time. He told Bāhiya that it was not the time for him to give his teaching. Not discouraged, Bāhiya pleaded a third time:

AIM OF THESE COMMENTARIES 37

- O Blessed One! It is difficult to predict the obstacles that may affect your life, or may affect my life. O Blessed One, please teach me the way. O Gone-to-Goodness One, please teach me the way, which may help me attain long lasting happiness and bliss.

The Buddha saw the fervent sincerity of Bāhiya and his eagerness to hear the teaching. He saw that this was the right time to deliver a sermon that was appropriate to Bāhiya's expectant state of mind. He deliberately delivered a brief sermon while Bāhiya was still prostrate, hands clasped, eagerly listening. The Buddha said:

- *In this case, Bāhiya, you should train yourself thus: "In what is seen, there is only what is seen; in what is heard, there is only what is heard; in what is sensed, there is only what is sensed; in what is cognized, there is only what is cognized". This is the way, Bāhiya, you should train yourself. Since for you, Bāhiya, in what is seen, there will be only what is seen; in what is heard, there will be only what is heard; in what is sensed, there will be only what is sensed; in what is cognized, there will be only what is cognized, therefore, Bāhiya, there is no you in connection with that. And since, Bāhiya, there is no you in connection with that, you will not be in this life, or hereafter, or in between the two. Thus, this is the end of suffering".*

The sutta went on: Through this brief teaching of the Blessed One, the mind of Bāhiya of the Bark Cloth was freed from mental defilements.

(Explanation: this means that, upon hearing the Buddha's teaching, Bāhiya attained the state of Arahat. He immediately had a deep cognitive understanding of the Truth. The Pāli texts call this state "khippābhiññānaṃ" which can be translated into "instantly comprehended the truth", or, using the Zen terminology, Bāhiya experienced a sudden and complete spiritual realization.)

Then, the Buddha continued on his alms round. Bāhiya bid the Buddha farewell... Shortly afterwards, a calf ran into him and killed him. After the midday meal, the Buddha was on his way back from his alms round with several other bhikkhus when he saw the deceased body of Bāhiya. The Buddha said to the bhikkhus:

- Bhikkhus, take the body of Bāhiya of the Bark Cloth, put it on a bier, cremate it, and build a memorial mound above it. Bhikkhus, one of your *fellows in the Holy Life* has passed away!

(Explanation: *Fellow in the Holy Life* means a person who shares the same code of conduct of the holy life as the disciples of the Buddha.)

The sutta went on: After the bhikkhus did exactly as the Buddha instructed, they came back to report to the Buddha and asked the Buddha to explain the case of Bāhiya.

The Buddha proclaimed to the congregated bhikkhus:

- Bhikkhus, Bāhiya of the Bark Cloth was a wise man who correctly practiced the dhamma in accordance with the dhamma, and did not trouble me with arguments about the dhamma. Bhikkhus, Bāhiya of the Bark Cloth has entered nibbāna.

The chain links that lead to spiritual realization

Explanation: The case of sudden and complete spiritual realization of Bāhiya was due to the following conditions.

AIM OF THESE COMMENTARIES 39

1. Docile mind

Bāhiya had a very pure mind when he lived on the sea shore of Suppāraka. His mind was not attached to possessions or material wealth whereas he was previously captivated by these. He lived the simple life, was contented with what he had, and maintained a pure conduct similar to the conduct of holy persons. For this reason, he was revered by the villagers as a person who lived the Holy Life. This indicated that his mind had become docile. It no longer aimlessly bustled around or got agitated in response to external causal conditions. This was the reason why he thought he had attained the state of Arahat or had entered the path to become an Arahat.

2. Doubt arising

But a heavenly being informed him that he was not on the path to become an Arahat. The heavenly being advised him to go to Sāvatthi to meet the Buddha and receive his teaching so that he could follow the correct path of Arahat-hood and attain Arahat-hood. It was then that he realized that he had misjudged the achievement level of his spiritual practice. The Buddha was a person who was following the correct path of Arahat-hood. The Buddha lived in Sāvatthi and he should go there promptly to pay his respects to the Buddha and seek his teaching.

3. Great doubt

He then resolved to go to Sāvatthi. He managed to cover the long distance in just one night. During his journey through the night, a single question filled his mind: how to attain long lasting happiness and bliss. This question grew in his mind into a great doubt which he hoped to resolve when he met the Buddha. This point was the foundation of his spiritual realization.

4. Growing the doubt

When he met the Buddha, a sense of joy welled up in his mind. He expressed his fervent plea to receive the Buddha's teaching. He considered that there was no time to spare as, if either the Buddha or he died, he would lose the opportunity to learn the teaching that would lead to his liberation. As he said: *"O Blessed One, it is difficult to predict the obstacles that may affect your life, or may affect my life."* However, the Buddha twice declined his fervent plea. Bāhiya did not get discouraged and pleaded a third time.

5. Opportune causal conditions

At that moment, the Buddha recognized Bāhiya's fervor and his yearning to hear the Buddha's teaching. The Buddha also knew that his mind was totally empty and was waiting for the Buddha to pour into it the appropriate words that would help him attain enlightenment or long lasting happiness and bliss. The Buddha recognized that causal conditions were all present and agreed to give him his teaching.

Bāhiya was filled with joy, and was ready to still his mind to receive the brief teaching of the Buddha. At that moment, he was listening with his wordless Ultimate Cognitive Awareness faculty.

6. Resolving the great doubt

Upon hearing the teaching, Bāhiya immediately attained a spiritual realization and became an Arahat.

AIM OF THESE COMMENTARIES 41

The Buddha proclaimed to the congregated bhikkhus that Bāhiya had attained a sudden and complete spiritual realization.

7. *Principle of sensory experience*

The key point of the brief sutta was to highlight the principle of sensory experience: when the senses experience something, we should let them experience it without any interference from the egoistic self. We could attain spiritual realization if we knew how to use this principle.

In the sutta, the Buddha said: *"In what is seen, there is only what is seen; in what is heard, there is only what is heard; in what is sensed, there is only what is sensed; in what is cognized, there is only what is cognized".*

In this passage, the Buddha taught us to recognize the four ultimate faculties that constitute the Wordless Awareness Mind and Buddha-Mind.

"In what is seen, there is only what is seen". When our eyes come into contact with an external object, there should only be the Ultimate Seeing faculty in action. The "self" should not be present. If the "self" is present, the seeing will no longer be objective. It no longer is seeing things as they are but becomes the "I see". This latter is a seeing where the "self" has inserted itself.

"In what is heard, there is only what is heard". This refers to the Ultimate Hearing faculty. When we hear, we should only hear and not make any reasoning about the content of the sound that we hear.

"In what is sensed, there is only what is sensed". This means that when we touch, only the Ultimate Touch faculty is present and not any interpretation about what is touched.

"In what is cognized, there is only what is cognized". In this sentence, the Buddha taught us that when we cognize something, we just maintain a state of wordless cognitive awareness and do not add any other content. In other words we have a bare cognition of the object.

"Therefore, Bāhiya, there is no you in connection with that". This sentence means that this state does not have a "self". For this state is the state of objective and silent awareness of the Wordless Awareness Mind where the "self" is not present.

"You will not be in this life, or hereafter, or in between the two. Thus, this is the end of suffering." This sentence means that if Bāhiya achieved the four above-mentioned states, he would attain liberation in this life. This means that, since he attained a sudden and complete spiritual realization of the No-Self principle, he had become an Arahat and would not be reborn in another life.

COMMENTARY TREATISE 3:

SIGNIFICANCE OF

THE SUBJECT OF THIS BOOK

Significance of the Subject of Zen and Contemporary Knowledge

Introduction

Before we go into the details of the various commentary treatises in question and answer format, I would like to develop in turn the two main topics of this book, Zen and Contemporary Knowledge.

First, I would like to explain the meaning of the term Zen which is commonly used as a synonym of Buddhist meditation. This is to avoid any misconceptions that arise from the use of the term "meditation" in religious circles or non-religious mainstream groups. Examples are terms such as Yoga Meditation, or Out-of-Body Meditation. Furthermore, there are several schools of Buddhism that use the terms Zen or "meditation" in their method of practice. Examples are: Zen Patriarchs Meditation, Mahāyāna Meditation, Zen Buddhism, Vipassanā Meditation, Mantra Meditation, Silent Meditation, Koan Meditation, Hua-Tou (Speech Exhaustion) Meditation, etc. This is why I would like to clarify the nature of the meditation that I am practicing.

The meditation that I teach is Early Buddhism meditation, which is the meditation taught by the Buddha when he was alive and taught until approximately 100 years after his passing. This is the meditation method that existed before Buddhism was split into the Doctrine of Elders school and the Great Congregation school.

I will quote from the suttas that describe the meditation method that the Buddha used to practice, to attain his spiritual realization and then enlightenment. He subsequently taught to both ordained and lay disciples what he had actually realized.

The Buddha's main didactic method is to teach according to each person's level of spiritual development. He considered that people can be divided into three categories: people of high level of spiritual development, people of medium level of spiritual development and people of low level of spiritual development. To people of high level of spiritual development, he taught the Ultimate Truth, which is the teaching beyond words. To people of medium and low spiritual development, he taught the Conventional Truth, which is the teaching with words.

In this book, I will explain and comment on the core points of the Buddha's teaching in a simple, easy to understand and non-specialist manner and reconcile them with scientific knowledge so that all of us can understand them.

Most significantly, the Buddha categorized the levels of spiritual realization according to the energy of the four ultimate faculties: (1) Ultimate Seeing, (2) Ultimate Hearing, (3) Ultimate Touch, and (4) Ultimate Cognitive Awareness. He attributed the first three ultimate faculties to the holy person's mind, and the fourth to the Tathā-Mind.

I will, in general, refer to the teaching of the Buddha in the Nikāya to explain the meditation terminology. I have occasionally used the question and answer format to make things clearer.

THE ESSENCE OF BUDDHIST MEDITATION

Origin of Zen

Meditation is nowadays a practice method widely spread to all parts of the world, but it originated in India. India has had many methods of meditation however there are two main types: Yoga Meditation and Buddhist Meditation. Yoga Meditation appeared about 500 years before the Buddha and was later documented by Patañjali. Buddhist Meditation was taught by the Buddha some 2500 years ago.

This book is a study on Buddhist Meditation, and therefore we will focus on this form of meditation.

What is Zen?

In order to gain a general understanding of the terms Zen or "meditation" from a Buddhist perspective, we need first to go back to the origin of the term "meditation" in the context of Buddhism in India. The reason is that meditation has deep roots in spiritual life in India. In Buddhism, there are two terms that are used to indicate meditation:

1. Jhāna: this is a Pāli term, the language used in the texts of Early Buddhism. This term means contemplative reflection, concentration of the mind, absorption of the mind (into an object).

The term "Jhāna" has its etymologic origin in "Jhāyati", which means *to contemplate*, or *to meditate* about a given subject. In this context, *jhāna* refers to the practice of Contemplation. Furthermore, *jhāna* is also related to the verb *jhāpeti*, which means *to burn* or *to eliminate* the defilements of the mind that impede the development of peace, serenity, and insight. However, *jhāna* requires the practitioner to attain *samādhi* in order for them to "burn" or "eliminate" their mental defilements. For only *samādhi* can create the conditions to *burn* or *eliminate* mental defilements.

SIGNIFICANCE OF THIS BOOK'S SUBJECT 47

The Buddha wanted to help the practitioner experience first awareness (pajānāti) as the main aim of this practice.

2. Dhyāna: this is a Sanskrit term, the language used in the texts of Developmental Buddhism. This term means *meditation, contemplation, reflection,* in particular turning the light on oneself or on a given practice topic; it also means the *state of mental concentration* on an object in order to merge the concept of the self and the object into a unified entity. At this point, there only subsists a stream of wordless awareness without the presence of the Thinking Faculty, the differentiating Consciousness or the reasoning Intellect.

The etymologic origin of *dhyāna* is the verb *dhyai*, which means *to think of; to contemplate; to meditate on; to recollect* a subject.

The two terms *jhāna* and *dhyāna* are the names given to a spiritual practice that applies in the four postures, especially the sitting posture. This spiritual practice originated in India and was established by the Buddha. It pertains to the four practices of Contemplation (Anupassanā), Tranquility (Samatha), Stillness of Mind (Samādhi), and Wisdom (Paññā). The purpose of this spiritual practice is to help the practitioner attain the four stages of *awareness, awakening, spiritual realization* and *inner realization* or *seeing one's true self, permanently living in wordless awareness, attaining freedom from concern,* and *liberation.*

The Chinese initially phonetically translated the terms *jhāna* and *dhyāna* into "Ch'an-na". Vietnamese monks then phonetically translated *Ch'an-na* into "Thiền Na". When the Chinese dropped the "na" ending to leave only "Ch'an", the Vietnamese did likewise. *Ch'an* was then phonetically translated by the Japanese into "Zen". On the other hand,

Western scholars translated *jhāna* and *dhyāna* into "meditation" according to their meaning.

In the last half-century, the two terms "Zen" and "meditation" have been used by Western scholars to translate *jhāna* or *dhyāna*. Fundamentally, the term "meditation" does not reflect the meaning of the two original terms *jhāna* or *dhyāna*. The most proximate purpose of *jhāna* or *dhyāna* is to help the practitioner attain samādhi which is founded upon the *unified mind*, and cannot be achieved by sitting and meditating, or playing a chasing game with thoughts, or turning the probing light of the intellect inward (reflection), as beginners do when they start their spiritual practice. Furthermore, the ultimate purposes of *jhāna* or *dhyāna* is seeing one's true self, spiritual realization, inner realization, attaining freedom from concern, and liberation. This is the reason why many modern Western meditators, once they have experienced the effect of meditation on their body, mind, and spiritual wisdom, use the terms Zen, or Zen Buddhism, or Buddhist Zen as translations of *jhāna* and *dhyāna* instead of the term "meditation" that was commonly used previously.

From a practical viewpoint, *jhāna* or *dhyāna* are specialized terms that indicate a spiritual practice in the four postures of walking, standing, lying, and sitting that is used in the four schools of Buddhism: Early Buddhism, Theravāda Buddhism, Developmental Buddhism and Zen Buddhism. If we seriously apply the Buddhist meditation method, we will realize that it has the capacity to help people attain:

1. A transformation of the mind.

2. An alleviation of illnesses of the body.

3. A harmonious balance between body and mind.

SIGNIFICANCE OF THIS BOOK'S SUBJECT 49

4. A development of spiritual wisdom.

5. A freedom from concern in this life, and freedom from concern when leaving this world, which is ultimate liberation.

Nowadays, *jhāna* and *dhyāna* (which we shall call "Zen" in this book) have a profound impact on the life of many progressive people in advanced Western countries and in countries with an Eastern cultural tradition. Zen is now understood in a broader sense in light of its effect. It no longer merely means the practices of breathing, samatha (tranquility) or anupassanā (contemplation) but also encompasses samādhi (stillness of mind) and paññā (wisdom). It not only helps people alleviate the dysfunctions in their body and mind, but can also create a harmonious balance between their body and mind, and help them develop their spiritual wisdom to a higher level. It not only eradicates the reasoning habits of the Intellect, disorganized thinking habits of the Thinking Faculty, and differentiating habits of the Consciousness, but also allows the Wordless Awareness Mind to emerge and become for the meditator a permanent awareness energy in the four postures. It not only allows the Wordless Awareness Mind to become a witness between the Consciousness and the senses, but it also forms a *catalytic process* that allows Buddha-nature to emerge and develop. For, although Buddha-nature is innate in every being, it could stay dormant if the Consciousness, Intellect and Thinking Faculty are always present.

In the words of Zen Master Thích Thanh Từ, "Zen is a spiritual science". This science is different from worldly science in as much as it goes deep into our Wordless Awareness Mind to exploit the *potential for spiritual realization* that is innate to the three ultimate faculties of the Wordless Awareness Mind, and deep into our Buddha-nature to exploit its *potential for enlightenment*. On the other hand, worldly science goes deep into our Consciousness, Thinking Faculty and Intellect to develop worldly knowledge. With this latter knowledge, humans are always faced with dualism, attachment and clinging to things (as if they are real). Sorrow and suffering, conflict and hatred will never disappear from their mind.

With the knowledge that derives from Buddha-nature, the mind will reach its ultimate liberation. Sorrow and suffering, conflict and hatred will end by themselves. Great compassion, great loving-kindness, great sympathetic joy and great equanimity will permanently manifest in our mind.

Two fundamental Zen traditions: spiritual realization and inner realization

Over a period of six long years, the Buddha successively progressed through various arduous practice stages with the aim of finding a way to:

- terminate the causes that lead to endless sorrow, suffering, birth and death,
- find a way to attain *the Unborn*,

but he reached an impasse.

He eventually remembered the breathing method that he discovered when he was a 10-year old child at the Ceremonial Plowing of the Land festivities conducted by his father, King Suddhodana. On that occasion, he sat under a rose-apple (jambu) tree and started breathing. He attained

SIGNIFICANCE OF THIS BOOK'S SUBJECT 51

the state of *automatic breathing* or *"pure breathing"* that led to a completely tranquil mind. He recalled his old experience, and re-applied the breathing method step by step. As a result, his mind reached a state of stable tranquility. Although his ears still heard the sounds of the surrounding environment and his eyes still saw objects that were in front of him, his mind did not get attached to these external conditions. He felt joyful, at ease. He experienced a sense of elation and bliss, which was the first result that he attained when he applied the awareness of the in-breath and out-breath method. He then progressed, step by step, deeper into the second stage of samādhi where all pondering, reflection and discursive thinking ended. Finally he went beyond Equanimity Samādhi and dwelt in Right Awareness. In that state, he realized, on the last night of the fourth week, that Craving Desire is the cause of the endless cycle of birth and death. That was his first spiritual realization. He did not stop at this stage and continued to dwell in Right Awareness (also called Immobility Samādhi or Diamond Samādhi). In his eighth week at the foot of the bodhi tree, he realized the true characteristics and essential nature of worldly phenomena that no-one had insofar recognized as clearly. Finally, he attained the ultimate enlightenment called Perfect Universal Enlightenment. At that point, he experienced a transformation previously unknown in his body, mind, and spiritual wisdom. This is what is called inner experience, a transformation that pervades the body, mind, and spiritual wisdom.

The Buddha felt compassion for all human beings living under constant delusion and addiction to the transitory mirages of worldly phenomena, continuing to be flung about in the sea of birth and death, and experiencing endless sorrow and suffering. For this reason, he decided to teach the dhamma to save humanity. Before he started his teaching journey, he reconstructed the process by which he attained spiritual realization and self-experience into a systematic and graded practice approach.

The successful example of the Buddha and his teaching method show that Buddhist meditation is based upon two fundamental principles: *spiritual realization* and *inner experience (or self-experience)*. Unlike Western philosophies, it is not based upon *thinking* or *intellectual reasoning*. For this reason, despite going through many momentous societal changes and rising and falling over the last 25 centuries, Buddhist meditation has endured. These two principles represent the fundamental and traditional values of Buddhist meditation.

If one tries to use thinking to approach Zen, one will find that this Zen will not be able to satisfy the practical needs of humanity through the ages. This Zen will only be able to subsist within a limited time period, and will be later eliminated. This is because thinking is the product of the subjective reasoning of the egoistic self. This reasoning is always based upon past information. It is a collection of disparate knowledge that was experienced and then recorded in memory or written in texts. It is not a knowing that arises spontaneously and immediately. For these reasons, it is only able to accord with people's mind in a given time period. When it is no longer appropriate, people will no longer accept it.

On the other hand, a spiritual realization is an intuitive insight that arises instantaneously from Buddha-nature, which resides in the precuneus. It is something that *was not known previously*, but now is known and recognized as clearly as if it is there in front of our eyes. It has the effect of re-balancing the body, transforming the mind, and

SIGNIFICANCE OF THIS BOOK'S SUBJECT 53

allowing transcendental wisdom to spring forth. For this reason, it remains relevant to humanity through the ages. For humans need it at all times.

A spiritual realization is fundamentally a product of our Wordless Awareness Mind and Buddha-nature, and not of our egoistic self. It is considered a catalyst that triggers the ushering of inner experience. Inner experience cannot occur without the catalytic effect of a spiritual realization. The more there are spiritual realizations, the broader and deeper the inner experience.

What is inner experience?

Inner experience means the transmutations or transformations of the body, mind, and spiritual wisdom that practitioners experience when they apply the correct method and technique. Any meditation practitioner who has once experienced a spiritual realization, even if it is a "minor" one, can experience a transformation of their body, mind, and spiritual wisdom.

This is the reason why spiritual realization is considered a catalyst for inner experience. A sufficient condition for spiritual realization is *stopping the thinking*. When thinking stops, so does the inner mental chatter and immediately the Wordless Awareness Mind comes to the fore. If we continuously think about a topic, inner mental chatter constantly occurs and makes it impossible for the Wordless Awareness Mind to be present. Therefore, the main objective of Zen is to *stop the thinking*. Once we manage to stop our thinking, the Wordless Awareness Mind instantaneously becomes present. This is the technique by which we activate our Wordless Awareness Mind, or the technique to attain a spiritual realization. In reality, it is not that our Wordless Awareness Mind was asleep or obscured by the veil of ignorance. It is us – our egoistic self – that is constantly present through our nebulous, purposeless, aimlessly agitated and disorganized thinking, and thus prevents our wordless, permanent and synchronous awareness from being present. Once we have awakened our Wordless Awareness Mind, making it present over short periods of time (a few minutes) or longer, while we repeatedly practice meditation in our walking, standing, lying, and sitting postures, we will have this *inner experience* in our body, mind, and spiritual wisdom.

Regarding our mind, we will start to realize that:

- We no longer have these bad habits that we have previously been attached or addicted to, such as gambling, smoking, drinking, or lying, etc.

- The attachment, addiction, and infatuation to the five desires (money, sex, fame, food, rest), which have previously permeated deep into our mind, are losing their powerful hold on our mind.

- The clinging to the reality of the self, clinging to the reality of phenomena, and clinging to our own perspective, which are afflictions that we previously could never shake off, suddenly no longer appear in our mind when we come into contact with society or people around us.

Regarding our body, we start to see clear changes:

- From a dark, somber, and sad complexion we now have an inner radiance that glows on our face as a fresh, bright, joyful and pure expression.

- Some leg, arm, head, face, eye, and mouth gestures naturally disappear from our demeanor when we walk, stand, lie, sit, and talk, such as: a frown, a grimace, a scowl; the absence of an innocent smile; sideways glances, eyes darting around; leg shaking, foot tapping, exaggerated hand and foot movement when talking; talking too much, talking over other people; arrogance and conceit.

- Deportments that are hurried, agitated, over solicitous, lacking dignity; behaviors that are impolite, un-courteous, inconsiderate, unsympathetic, unforgiving; conduct that is impure, immoral, against religious precepts gradually disappear owing to the change in our mind without us even noticing.

- Furthermore, our physical constitution is getting stronger and healthier. Our body will have the ability to cure itself from illnesses such as asthma, stomach ulcers, irregular heartbeat, high or low blood pressure, etc.

Regarding our spiritual wisdom, we will understand clearly what the Buddha said in the suttas and what the Buddhist Patriarchs said in commentaries. We will especially develop seeing and knowing things as they are: when we come into contact with phenomena, we will see and know them as they are without interference from the reasoning of the Intellect or the dualistic thinking and differentiation of the Consciousness. This knowing-and-seeing-things-as-they-are originates from the intuitive and the analytical knowing faculty of our Wordless Awareness Mind.

If we practice assiduously to allow our Wordless Awareness Mind to be continuously present in all four postures of Zen practice, in particular the sitting posture, we will one day experience self-generated wisdom.

This is the fundamental characteristic of Zen that, as someone who has just begun the Zen journey, we need to focus on. This is the path that leads us straight to our objective. It shows that practicing Zen is not about playing a chasing game with our thoughts, nor is it about idle and vague reasoning. On the contrary, it is about aiming straight toward our Wordless Awareness Mind (which consists of Ultimate Seeing, Ultimate Hearing and Ultimate Touch) and our Buddha-nature (or Ultimate Cognitive Awareness), which is located in the precuneus.

Zen's main objective

Through the teaching direction adopted by the Buddha, we can see that the objective of Zen is to serve humanity. This is a humanity that is still attached to four worldly layers often called by the Buddha the four layers of mental defilements.

"Mental defilements" is a translation of the Pāli term *āsava*. It means a "secretion" or "outflow". The main meanings of *āsava* are: thoughts that poison the mind; an intoxicant; an addiction; a taint; an infatuation; a defilement; a corruption; a mania. They consist of four groups: ignorance defilements, desire defilements, craving for existence defilements; and false perspective defilements. If seriously and correctly practiced, Zen has the capacity to eliminate each layer of mental defilements from our karma-consciousness. The four layers of mental defilements are the causes of rebirth as well as ephemeral happiness and peace in life, in which sorrow, suffering, grievance, hatred, conflict, greed, anger, and delusion are ever present. Once mental defilements are eliminated, our mind will be transformed, steady, and stable; our body will be strong and healthy; our spirit will be expanded and clear. Passions, addictions, infatuations, and attraction to worldly pleasures will no longer be obstacles in our daily life. Bliss and happiness will then really be ever present in our daily life and that of our family.

Zen's fundamental characteristic

When we truly live with Zen (and not just practicing it in an amateurish way or following it as a vogue) we will be able to taste inner experience. We will then realize that Zen has the capacity to transform the nature of our body, mind, and consciousness and make our insights and wisdom blossom. It is able to achieve this feat without the need for dogma and morals, or memorizing meditation teaching tapes, or cumbersome religious ceremonies such as sutta reciting, wooden altar bell striking, prayer beads counting or other complex rituals. On the contrary, practicing Zen consists simply of using a sensory response to awaken the Wordless Awareness Mind or one of its three ultimate faculties (Ultimate Seeing, Ultimate Hearing, and Ultimate Touch) and an intrinsically-generated response to awaken the Ultimate Cognitive Awareness faculty. This is the fundamental characteristic of Zen. If we deviate from this crucial point, we will never be able to experience spiritual realization and inner experience. This is the reason why Zen teaches us to go straight and not in a circle; to aim straight at the goal and not meander around it; to seek true bliss and not temporary and ephemeral happiness.

Fundamental obstacle on the Zen path

The Zen practitioner may encounter many obstacles, however foremost of these is the *speech formation* mental process which consists of Inner Talk (*vitakka*) and Inner Dialogue (*vicāra*). Inner Talk and Inner Dialogue are the silent talk and silent dialogue that occur in our mind. If we sit in meditation but still have silent inner talk and silent inner dialogue in our mind, the tranquility of mind (*samatha*) and stillness of mind (*samādhi*) will not be present. If we let this happen, we will never achieve our goals of attaining bliss, freedom from concern and development of spiritual wisdom, even though we may spend many years practicing Zen and wear out many meditation cushions. This is a crucial point that those who have just started on the Zen path need to appreciate. If they don't, they may waste a lifetime of spiritual practice.

Conclusion

This commentary treatise explains that the most important point in Zen is to *keep the mental chatter under control*. If we cannot control our mental chatter, even for just a few seconds, our Zen practice will reach an impasse. Inner Talk and Inner Dialogue will constantly appear in our mind. If we persist in this practice, we will be a Zen practitioner in name only, and will never experience the fruits of Zen which are freedom from suffering, enlightenment, and liberation from birth and death.

Our Wordless Awareness Mind becomes present when our mental chatter ceases and becomes silent. If the mental chatter remains active, thoughts will never quieten down.

SIGNIFICANCE OF THIS BOOK'S SUBJECT

I hope that you have grasped the essence of this commentary treatise. I will now continue with a commentary treatise on contemporary knowledge.

Significance of contemporary knowledge

To address the topic of contemporary knowledge, I will use a hypothetical situation where someone asks me questions so that I can provide clear answers.

Question: Master, could you please tell us what you mean by contemporary knowledge?

Answer: The contemporary knowledge that I refer to is the state of human knowledge of our era.

Question: And what are the characteristics of the era we are living in?

Answer: The era that we are living in, in brief, is the era of science and technology. This means that anything that pertains to our life is included in the scope of science and technology, such as: culture, society, security, health, neuroscience, Zen studies, and Buddhist studies, etc.

Historical background

Science and technology have existed in the past in human civilizations. They have helped humans achieve ever more progress in their life.

Science as a discipline has developed and continues to develop in countries with a high level of culture and civilization.

Developmental Buddhism has the concept of the "Five Branches of Learning": Dhamma Knowledge, Discursive

Knowledge, Language Knowledge, Technical Knowledge, and Medical Knowledge.

Question: Master, could you please explain further the Five Branches of Learning?

Answer: There is a Buddhist tradition that holds that a person who wishes to teach the dhamma needs to be equipped with the Five Branches of Learning or five types of knowledge:

- Dhamma knowledge: knowledge of the Buddhist suttas.

- Discursive knowledge: knowledge of reasoning methods.

- Language knowledge: knowledge of language, literature.

- Technical knowledge: knowledge of technology and craft.

- Medical knowledge: medical and pharmacological knowledge.

Question: And Master, what is technology?

Answer: Technology is a subject that requires from each individual three fundamental abilities:

- Have an average level of education that enables the understanding of information related to the profession or trade at the center of the problem that the person is endeavoring to resolve.

- Have a creative mind.

- Have the ability to come up with new ideas.

Question: Master, do we need to have scientific knowledge when we practice Zen?

Answer: Very much so. When we practice Zen, we need to equip ourselves with scientific knowledge, more specifically neuroscience knowledge.

Question: Master, why does the Zen practitioner need to know neuroscience?

Answer: The reason is that, when we practice Zen, everything that we do affects the brain. We need to know the location, function, and characteristics of the various areas of the brain so that we can discern when we are practicing correctly and when we are not. In particular, what are the effects when we practice correctly and what are they when we practice incorrectly.

Further Reading 2: Tangible Benefits of Contemporary Knowledge

Brief Overview of the Structure and Functions of and Interactions between Endocrine Glands within the Human Body

1. *The endocrine system*

The endocrine system consists of a number of glands that *do not secrete their biochemicals through ducts* but instead directly into the blood stream. These biochemicals are then carried by the circulatory system throughout the body.

The scientific term for these biochemicals is *"hormone"*. The term hormone has a Greek etymology that means "to excite", "to urge", or "an activator". There are several hormone-secreting glands inside the body, and as they are all directly related to the hypothalamus and pituitary gland, endocrinologists have grouped them together as a system.

The primary function of endocrine glands is to secrete *hormones*. The role of hormones is to *regulate the metabolism* of other cells within the body as well as other functions such as tissue growth or organ illnesses when the mind is destabilized by terror, anxiety, anger, fear, despondency, sorrow, worry, stress or any other emotional state generated by the nervous system.

Conversely, hormones have also the capacity to *balance the inner energy* of the Zen practitioner when they correctly practice the Zen methods of samatha (tranquility), anupassanā (contemplation), samādhi (stillness of mind) and paññā (wisdom). This mechanism shows the crucial role played by the nervous system through its close interaction with all other parts of the body. If we are able to regulate its function through the practice of Zen, it will indirectly interact with the endocrine system and help us improve our well-being.

2. *Structure and function of endocrine glands*

- The endocrine glands consist of:

Brief Overview of the Hypothalamus and Pituitary Gland

Introduction

The pair hypothalamus and pituitary gland (or hypophysis) has great influence on our health, illnesses, and in expressing our psychological and emotional states. When we seriously apply one of the four Zen methods of samatha (tranquility), anupassanā (contemplation), samādhi (stillness of mind) and paññā (wisdom), they have the capacity to improve our physical well-being, eliminate psychosomatic illnesses, and stabilize our mental and emotional well-being.

- Internal organ illnesses and psychosomatic illnesses have their origin in agitations of the mind, or in other words, in the central nervous system. If we know how to *regulate its attitude* (meaning that we regulate our own attitude), the paired hypothalamus/pituitary gland will secrete biochemical substances that are beneficial to our body.

- In our Zen practice, we need to understand the effects that the False Mind and the True Mind have on this pair. We will be able to ascertain the true value of practicing Zen using the correct method, the correct technique, and the correct appropriateness.

The hypothalamus is a small organ located inside the brain, behind the eyes, below the thalamus and above the pituitary gland. (The thalamus is the organ that receives stimuli from the five objects of the senses. It directly receives the signals sent from four sensory organs: eyes, ears, tongue, and body, while the smell signals from the nose travel first to the hypothalamus and then onto the thalamus.)

The pituitary gland is the gland that has the greatest influence on the endocrine system. Its activity is directed by the hypothalamus. The hypothalamus monitors the secretion of biochemical substances and receives information from other parts of the cerebral cortex to direct the secretion of hormones and neurotransmitters that regulate the functioning of other organs. These organs have in turn an influence back on the nervous system in a *feedback loop* that illustrates the close interaction between the nervous system, the endocrine glands, and all internal organs. Eventually, it is the nervous system that *bears the brunt* of events that it created in the mind: anxiety, fear, terror, utter despair, or un-ending sorrow... The central nervous system is both the conductor leading the orchestra, and the audience listening to the melodious or powerful music produced by the players.

The pituitary gland has two lobes:

1. The posterior lobe is under the control of two groups of nuclei in the hypothalamus. The first group of nuclei are supraoptic nuclei that direct the secretion of ADH (antidiuretic hormone). An excess of ADH will constrict the peripheral blood vessels resulting in high blood pressure. The second group of nuclei are paraventricular nuclei that act on the pituitary gland to produce oxytocin. This hormone stimulates the mammary glands

SIGNIFICANCE OF THIS BOOK'S SUBJECT

in women to produce milk for their baby after childbirth.

2. The anterior lobe plays an important role in activating a number of endocrine glands, and for this reason the pituitary gland is called the master gland. First, through vein capillaries linking it to the hypothalamus, it receives signals in the form of various neurotransmitters that the hypothalamus releases based on information it receives from the limbic system and the two pre-frontal cortexes. There are also instances where the hypothalamus receives information arising from the weather, from the air coming into contact with the body, and from the breath through its direct link with the nose.

The anterior lobe of the pituitary gland secretes five main types of hormones.

A. Growth hormone (GH). This hormone mainly aims at developing bones and skeletal muscles, resulting in the growth and lengthening of bones, the skeleton and muscles. An excess of GH will result in abnormal growth such as gigantism with body height over 2 m and up to 2.4 m. On the other hand, a deficiency in GH will result in dwarfism (body height from 70 cm to 1.2 m). An abnormal body growth is a sign of excessive GH. If we detect one, we should get an examination to see whether an operation to remove a tumor in the anterior pituitary is required. Otherwise we may display symptoms of acromegaly (excessive body growth): large chin, large nose, and coarse limbs. This is an illness.

B. Prolactin (PRL) hormone. This hormone triggers the production of milk from a woman's mammary glands after childbirth.

C. Thyroid-stimulating hormones (TSH). This biochemical substance aims straight at the thyroid gland located at the base of the neck, triggering it into secreting thyroid hormones. TSH contains a high level of glycoprotein.

D. Adrenocorticotropic hormones (ACTH). This hormone stimulates the outer cortex of the adrenal glands. When the pituitary gland receives the corticotropin-releasing hormone (CRH) from the hypothalamus, it secretes ACTH to stimulate the outer cortex of the adrenal glands into releasing several *corticosteroid* (corticoids) hormones that belong in two groups: cortisol (or glucocorticoids) and aldosterone (or mineralocorticoids).

Cortisol is most critical to our well-being, but it can also be very detrimental to our health. When released in excessive quantity, it can cause memory loss, etc.

Aldosterone is an important hormone that controls blood pressure and acts on the kidneys to reduce the quantity of salt lost in urine.

E. Gonadotropin (sexual regulating) hormones. When the anterior lobe of the pituitary gland receives the gonadotropin-releasing hormones (GnRH) from the hypothalamus, it in turn releases the gonadotropin hormones which consist of two hormones: FSH (follicle-stimulating hormone) and LH (luteinizing hormone) to regulate the function of gonads (sex glands) in both males and females. In females, FSH increases the development of eggs and stimulates the secretion of estrogen (females' sex hormone). In males, FSH triggers the production of semen in the testes. Meanwhile, LH increases the production of sex hormones for both sexes.

1. Pineal Gland. This is a small gland the size of a corn kernel, located inside the brain and joined to the roof of the thalamus. Its only function is to release the biochemical melatonin into the blood stream according to a day-night cycle over 24 hours. Melatonin is most abundant at night, and is at its lowest level between around 11 am and 1 p.m. The main characteristic of melatonin is to inhibit GnRH (gonadotropin-releasing hormone) production in males and females, and inhibit MSH (melanocyte-stimulating hormone) production in the anterior pituitary. When a person practices the *Looking at Sunlight-Moonlight* or *Looking at Light Bulb* exercises, their pineal gland will release higher levels of melatonin. The reason is that a short section of the optic nerve connects with the pineal gland. Therefore when one practices *looking at light* (sunlight, moonlight or light from a light bulb), the light received by the eyes stimulates the pineal gland into releasing serotonin. When serotonin is produced in high quantity, it becomes melatonin.

2. Pituitary Gland (or Hypophysis). This gland releases several hormones directly into the blood stream and is considered the master gland, the most important gland of the endocrine system. It is shaped like a pea and is linked to the hypothalamus through a funnel. The pituitary gland regulates and monitors the activity of the other endocrine glands. It consists of two lobes: the posterior lobe controlled by the nervous system, and the anterior lobe controlled by the hypothalamus.

3. Thyroid Gland. The thyroid gland is situated in front of the trachea, just below the throat. It is shaped like a shell, consists of two lobes and weighs about 34 grams on average. It produces hormones that are considered essential in the regulation of the body metabolism and plays an important role in maintaining blood pressure. Under the activation of the TSH (thyroid-stimulating hormone) from the anterior pituitary, the thyroid releases into the blood stream the hormone *thyroxine*, a hormone that contains four iodine atoms [T4] and is also called tetra-iodothyronine, and the hormone *tri-iodothyronine* which contains three iodine atoms [T3], in a ratio of about 90%-10%. It also releases the hormone *calcitonin* that plays an important role in regulating the level of calcium in the blood. Both T4 and T3 play a very important role in regulating the rate of metabolism in our body. This means that the rate at which the body converts the food that we eat into energy depends on these two hormones. If our body produces a high level of thyroxine, we will have good appetite; are not choosy about what we eat; and can eat all sorts of food. Our body will feel alert, reacts quickly and is full of energy. Conversely, a lack of thyroxine leads to feeling sleepy. We will sleep a lot but still feel like we are lacking sleep, and although we sleep a lot we will feel lethargic, tired. At the same time, our body does not cope well with the cold weather. When the rate of metabolism increases, heat energy will increase and helps us cope with the cold weather. Thyroxine is essential to the body growth and mental development of children.

In adults, a low level of thyroxine leads to symptoms of tiredness, dry skin, hair loss, weight gain, constipation, and not handling cold weather well. In children, it results in slow body and mental development.

When the Zen practitioner achieves the first stage of samādhi (stopping thoughts from arising for one to ten minutes), the hypothalamus releases the thyrotropin-releasing hormone (TRH) which stimulates the pituitary gland into releasing the thyroid-stimulating hormone

(TSH). TSH then stimulates the thyroid gland into releasing thyroxine. We will feel warmth rising from our two feet to our body, hands and face. If we manage to repeatedly stop thoughts for short periods of time (from one to ten minutes), the afflictions of depression, lethargy, restlessness, worry, and tiredness will disappear. When we reach deeper levels of samādhi, the rate of thyroxine release will be in harmonious balance and we will have a smooth and shiny skin.

An excessive level of thyroid hormones will result in tiredness, fatigue, anxiety, palpitation, perspiration, and weight loss even though one was eating well.

Calcitonin combines with hormones released by the parathyroid gland to regulate the level of calcium in the body.

4. Parathyroid Glands. They consist of four small bean-sized, oval-shaped glands that sit right against the two lobes of the thyroid gland. They release parathormone (PTH), a hormone rich in protein that helps regulate the level of calcium in the blood. Too little PTH leads to tetany (a constriction or contraction of muscles resulting in pain). Too much PTH results in excessive blood calcium leading to a weakened nervous system, which may show as abnormal reflex movements, weakened skeletal muscles and kidney stone formation.

5. Thymus. It consists of two lobes, a left one and a right one, sometimes further sub-divided into three or four lobes. The posterior area is enlarged and is called the base. The thymus has a yellow-brown color. Both the cortex and medulla of the thymus are filled with lymphocytes, commonly called "white blood cells", which play a crucial role in the immune system. The thymus lies beneath the sternum in the upper thorax, and links up with the trachea. The function of the thymus is to transform lymphocytes into "T-cells" which play an important role in the body's defense against viruses and other pathogens.

6. Adrenal Glands. They consist of two glands that are pyramidal in shape and situated above the two kidneys. Each gland consists of two parts: a cortex and a medulla. Both play an important role in the body's response to external stress through the release of biochemical substances such as *cortisol* and *epinephrine*. These substances result in changes to the heart rate, blood pressure, metabolism (which is the way the body stores energy and utilizes food) and other body functions in response to the change in the environment. However, when they reach certain levels, they will bring disorder to the individual's mood and behavior. Stress that reaches levels that the individual cannot bear will result in damage to the internal organs and muscular pains.

> A. Adrenal cortex. It consists of three separate areas. The outermost layer secretes the *aldosterone* hormone which acts on retaining sodium in urine and regulates water and minerals levels in the blood. For this reason, aldosterone is also called a *mineralocorticoid*. The middle and innermost layers secrete the hormone *hydrocortisone* (also called *cortisol*) and *corticosterone*, as well as a small quantity of the hormone *androgen* (that stimulates the development of male characteristics). Cortisol is a very important biochemical involved in the metabolism of glucose, fat, protein, and carbohydrates to help the body recover and increase blood sugar level. For this reason it is classified as a *gluco-corticosteroid*, a substance that increases circulatory glucose level. In addition, cortisol and

SIGNIFICANCE OF THIS BOOK'S SUBJECT

corticosterone strengthen the immune system and have an anti-inflammatory effect.

B. Adrenal medulla. When stimulated by sympathetic nerves, cells in the adrenal medulla release two hormones: *adrenaline* (also called *epinephrine*) and *noradrenaline* (also called *norepinephrine*). Adrenaline is the hormone that is secreted in response to signals from the sympathetic nervous system. These signals convey feelings of fear, anxiety and excessive sadness. It results in increased heart rate, increased blood sugar level, constriction of the blood vessels (resulting in higher blood pressure and higher heart rate), and diversion of blood flow toward the brain, heart, and skeletal muscles.

Noradrenaline, on the other hand, is secreted in response to feelings of anger, hatred, and aggression. It also plays an important role in heightening our arousal level to maintain vigilance and readiness to respond to circumstances. Thus, noradrenaline helps maintain blood pressure at a constant level.

7. **Pancreas.** Elongated and triangular in shape, the pancreas lies behind the stomach. Its head is surrounded by the concavity of the duodenum while its tail abuts the spleen. The pancreas consists almost entirely of exocrine cells and endocrine cells. Its endocrine cells secrete digestive enzymes that break down carbohydrates, fats, proteins, and sour food. Carbohydrates provide our body with energy and help us maintain good health. They are an essential group in our daily food intake and comprise cereals, vegetables, and starch.

The pancreas' endocrine cells secrete the hormones *insulin* and *glucagon*. These two hormones have opposite effects but they both work to keep the blood glucose level in balance. If the level of blood insulin is too low, the blood glucose level will increase, leading to diabetes (diabetes mellitus). Conversely, if the level of blood insulin is too high, the blood glucose level will fall, leading to chronic fatigue.

Insulin is a small protein consisting of 51 amino acids that is produced by the beta cells of the pancreas. It promotes the absorption of blood glucose into the liver and muscle cells as stores of energy for the body. Glucose is stored in the liver as glycogen. When we exercise or encounter a highly stressful situation, glycogen is transformed back into glucose to allow the body to face the situation (it becomes then a source of energy). Insulin prevents the accumulation of glucose in the blood and ensures that tissues have enough glucose.

Diabetes occurs when the pancreas manufactures too little or no insulin at all.

Glucagon is a polypeptide hormone consisting of 29 amino acids, and is produced by the alpha cells of the pancreas. It acts on the glycogen stored in the liver and muscles to transform it back into glucose. The glucose is then released into the blood stream and becomes a source of energy for all cells in the body. When the blood glucose level is low, glucagon is released by the pancreas to increase it. One unit of glucagon can release 100 million units of glucose into the blood stream. The main target of glucagon is the glycogen stored in the liver. From the liver, glucose is released into the blood stream.

Insulin and glucagon act in opposite directions. Too much glucagon leads to diabetes. Only insulin can balance glucagon.

8. Gonads (sex glands). They produce sperm in males and eggs in females. The hormone *gonadotropin* released by the pituitary gland regulates the activity of the gonads in males and females.

REFERENCES

In relation to endocrine glands, the pituitary gland and hypothalamus

1. Abercrombie, M., Hickman, M., Johnson, M. L. and Thain, M., *Dictionary of Biology*, pp. 179, 286, 446-447.

2. Bevan, James, *Pictorial Handbook of Anatomy and Physiology*, pp. 53, 56, 60, 61.

3. Carlson, John G. and Hatfield, Elaine, *Psychology of Emotion*, pp. 44, 130-131, 133-134, 136, 302, 379, 451-453, 488.

4. Considine, Douglas M. (editor), *Van Nostrand's Scientific Encyclopedia*, pp. 1154, 1662, 3092-3093.

5. Clayman, Charles B., *The American Medical Association, Encyclopedia of Medicine*, pp. 403, 562, 769.

6. Guyton, Arthur C., *Textbook of Medical Physiology*, pp. 678-679, 884-886, 917-918, 1003-1004

7. Marieb, Elaine N., *Human Anatomy and Physiology*, pp. 111, 392, 400, 540, 548.

8. Martini, Frederic, *Fundamentals of Anatomy and Physiology*, pp. 180, 371, 373, 469-498.

9. Myers, David G., *Exploring Psychology*, pp. 42-43, 275, 285.

10. Restak, Richard M., *The Brain*, pp. 16-18, 108, 122-132, 154, 224.

11. Rossi, Ernest L. and Cheek, David B., *Mind-Body Therapy*, pp. 165, 329, 463.

12. Silverstein, Alvin, *Human Anatomy and Physiology*, pp. 260, 275, 697-702.

13. Whitfield, Philip, *The Human Body Explained*, pp. 66, 84, 180.

COMMENTARY TREATISE 4:

A SPIRITUAL SCIENCE

A Spiritual Science

Introduction

Nowadays, Zen is considered a spiritual science as its ultimate aim is to help practitioners experience their spirituality. This spiritual experience differs from a religious experience in the following ways:

- Zen has the capacity to create a harmonious balance in the body and mind of the practitioner and alleviate their mental or psychosomatic illnesses without relying on the intake of external medicines. Nor does it need prayers for salvation from all Buddhas from the ten directions, or from all Boddhisattvas, or from deities as in other religions. Zen has the ability to exploit the "medicinal centers" inside our body and our brain.

- Zen has the capacity to exploit the energy of our Wordless Awareness Mind and our Buddha-nature. It can generate human energy fields.

- Zen helps us transform our bad karma into good karma.

For these reasons, we need to understand clearly the functions and processes of our brain when we study and practice Zen. We do not underestimate the value of scientific knowledge. We are living in the 21st century within an evolutionary trend centered on science. We need to use scientific knowledge to explain Zen's teaching and prove its value.

Zen is nowadays different from what it was in ancient times. We now have the means to combine and reconcile Zen with science to understand clearly the functions of, and effects on, various areas of the brain in the cerebral cortex

A SPIRITUAL SCIENCE

and limbic system. At the very least, advances in scientific knowledge have allowed us to have a tentative understanding of some functions of the brain. With this understanding, we will be able to avoid incorrect practices that lead to illnesses of the body, disturbances of the mind, disharmony with the surrounding environment, and inability to develop the energy of spiritual wisdom. If we do not understand the special functions of the brain, we will never believe that Zen is a spiritual science. It has the capacity to alleviate our psychosomatic illnesses, transform our mind and generate energies of harmony within ourselves and with the surrounding environment. It relies on our own effort in practice.

We are truly starting on a spiritual journey when we commit ourselves to Zen practice. This journey has three meanings:

1. We are travelling into a world about which we have no prior knowledge. Once we experience it, we will see that our insights and wisdom have truly opened up. We see many problems with more clarity than previously. We have many innovative ideas. Our complexion reflects an inner radiance. In Zen terminology, we have experienced a "spiritual realization", or "full spiritual realization".

2. As a result of a re-balancing of our body and transformation of our mind, we will experience in our own body and mind states of being healthy, energized, serene, joyful, and in harmony.

3. We officially declare war on all demons of thought, not by exerting effort in fighting them, but by progressively vanquishing them on the battlefield of our mind by

using the marvelous weapon of the "No Talk" technique.

Based on the experience of those who have gone on the path before, you will need six necessary pre-requisites before you start your spiritual journey if you want to succeed at alleviating illnesses of the body, transforming the mind, creating a harmonious balance between body and mind, and developing spiritual wisdom and altruism:

- awakening
- need
- direction
- means of travel
- meditation techniques and practical exercises
- assiduity and regular practice

Question: Master, could you please explain why having an *awakening* is the first pre-requisite?

Answer: The reason is that we need to make use of our Intellect when we start our practice. Awakening is a function of the Intellect. When the Intellect becomes awakened, it is no longer distorted and will lead the Thinking Faculty and Consciousness into becoming silent. The Intellect is the main instrument of the Thinking Faculty and Consciousness. When it has become awakened, the Thinking Faculty and Consciousness no longer have the means to be active.

When we apply the meditation techniques and practical exercises, I often highlight the awakening role of the

Intellect. The aim is to avoid using the Thinking Faculty and Consciousness when we practice.

When we use the Thinking Faculty, we often dredge up the past because its function is to think and ponder. When we use the Consciousness, we often become attached to the object in order to differentiate and compare.

Question: Master, could you please explain why having a *need* is an important condition for a person who wishes to enter the spiritual path?

Answer: In any human endeavor, we must first have a need for something if we want to be successful at it. For example, if we want to practice Zen, we must first have a need for an outcome from Zen, such as enhancing our physical health, or achieving peace of mind, or developing spiritual wisdom. Only then will we spend the effort and time to study and practice in order to achieve this outcome.

Question: Master, could you please explain what you mean by *direction*?

Answer: If you want to get to somewhere, you need to ascertain first the direction of travel. The direction is also the destination. When we know the direction of travel or the destination, we will not risk losing time by losing our way or going around in circles. If we lose our way on a physical journey, we can always retrace our steps. But when we lose our way on our spiritual journey, the consequences are more serious: our body may carry psychosomatic illnesses due to the over stimulation of our sympathetic nervous system. Furthermore, if we are the leader of a group of practitioners, the consequences are even more serious.

The correct direction in Zen practice is to aim at activating one of the three ultimate faculties of the Wordless Awareness Mind, or higher still, the wordless cognitive awareness faculty of our Buddha-nature (nowadays associated with the precuneus).

Question: Master, could you please explain what the *means of travel* in Buddhist Zen are?

Answer: There are four means of practice:

1. Using our awakened Intellect through the practice of single-thought awareness, either with words or without words

2. Silent awareness

3. Awake awareness

4. Cognitive awareness

Means of practice are practice topics that we use in our practice to activate our Wordless Awareness Mind to isolate our false mind and false thoughts and stimulate the ultimate faculties of the Wordless Awareness Mind. Most importantly, they help re-balance the activity of the hypothalamus. It is through the hypothalamus that the states of our False Mind or True Mind are manifested externally as gestures, facial expressions, eye expressions, smiles, sadness, joy, anger, resentment, anxiety, worry, sorrow, fear, words, and tone of voice.

The hypothalamus transmits signals to the cerebral cortex, to various neuronal systems, and to the endocrine system to get these areas to respond in accordance with our emotional states. For this reason, we can easily fail if we apply the correct method and the correct means of practice but do not know the appropriate practical exercises and meditation techniques. Instead of leading us to a healthy body, peaceful mind and clear knowledge and wisdom, we end up with a more unhealthy body, a more attached mind, and less knowledge and wisdom. We use the reasoning Intellect or Consciousness instead of the awakened Intellect to support our practice.

Question: Master, could you please explain what are the *practical exercises* and *meditation techniques* in Zen practice?

Answer: Practical exercises are simple exercises that help us experience a peaceful mind and achieve a state of samatha (tranquility), whereas a meditation technique is a more important and profound way of practice that aims at terminating the mental chatter, taking control of our thinking in a stable way, and experiencing samādhi (stillness of mind).

Question: Master, could you please explain what you mean by *assiduous and regular* practice?

Answer: Buddhist texts often mention "assiduous practice". We should establish a daily schedule of practice and strictly adhere to it. For example we set for ourselves 15 minutes of practice every day early in the morning and in the evening before bed, and then progressively increase the amount of time.

Question: Master, could you please explain why we need to practice regularly?

Answer: Meditation is a method to train our neurons into having a new habit, which is the habit of silence. We have from birth developed for our neurons the habit of agitation by having verbal chatter in our mind all the time, day and night, even in our sleep. This is why we need to patiently practice regularly every day to establish a new habit of silence for our mind.

In conclusion, if you come to Zen without being truly awakened, you will not feel that you need Zen. You will never follow the Zen path to its completion. I consider awakening to be a necessary condition, whereas having a need for an outcome of Zen is like a goal that we are aiming for. It also gives us the direction of travel. We will then need the means of travel to get to where to want to be. Without practice, we will never get there. However, we need to choose a practice that is suitable to our capacity, and we need to choose a method that accords with our need. For example we may choose a practice to alleviate insomnia, and a different one to alleviate cardio vascular problems.

The other important thing is regular practice. One needs to set aside two formal daily practice sessions. Each session should last 15 to 30 minutes, or more. There are other opportunities for practice such as driving to work; breaks at work; lunch time at work; passing water; brushing one's teeth; having a shower or bath; doing the laundry, etc.

Zen is a Spiritual Science

1. *Practical purpose*

Nowadays, we need to be clear that Zen is a spiritual science.

First, Zen is a science because it has clear definitions, clear systems of practice that go straight to the point, and clear

A SPIRITUAL SCIENCE 85

direct and indirect relationships between mind, teaching, brain, and body.

These relationships establish a mutual interaction between mind, teaching, brain, and body, where the mind plays the most important role. The term "mind" is used here in a narrow sense to mean the awakened Intellect.

When we apply the practical exercises and meditation techniques, we activate the limbic system, which in turn causes the endocrine system and autonomic nervous system to secrete biochemical substances.

When we practice, we are actually applying the principle of sensory response, i.e. we are using one of the five sense organs in our practice. Under this process, when our sense organs come into contact with an object, two areas are stimulated:

1. The parasympathetic nervous system, which then triggers a series of reactions in the brain, endocrine glands, and internal organs.

2. One of the ultimate faculties of the Wordless Awareness Mind. During this process, false thoughts from the pre-frontal cortex become isolated, and the True Mind emerges. At the same time, the limbic system of the brain is activated by the Wordless Awareness Mind.

Whether our internal organs are re-balanced or not will depend on the cascading interaction between the mind, teaching, Wordless Awareness Mind (one of the three ultimate faculties), the limbic system, the parasympathetic nervous system, and the endocrine system.

Second, Zen is a science because Zen's focus is to help people have a new perspective on worldly phenomena, on the principle of action and effect in Zen and on the cascading interaction between the mind, teaching, brain, and biochemical substances secreted in the body. Zen does not generate delusions or hallucinations in the practitioner. On the contrary, it brings the practitioner into the world or reality.

Third, Zen is a science because Zen does not promote cumbersome religious rituals or prayers to deities, Buddhas, or Bodhisattvas for salvation. The Zen practitioner projects the image of a *lone traveller* who sits in the meditation hall with eyes half-closed and back straight but is full of an inner energy, determination, dignity, and tranquility that radiates out, while practicing a samādhi topic.

I call Zen "spiritual" because, first, Zen aims at developing the innate creative energy of the ultimate faculties of the Wordless Awareness Mind, and not the energy of the Consciousness. When we use the energy of the Consciousness, we can never stop the mental chatter and dualistic thinking, nor can we reach the Unborn-knowledge that the Buddha attained and imparted to posterity.

Furthermore, if the energy of the Consciousness continues to heighten, the egoistic self will never become tranquil and pure and the Tathā-Mind will never become a reality in our mind.

Armed with this new perspective, people will be able to recognize the precious value of the teaching of the Buddha and Buddhist Patriarchs and apply it in their daily life. They will become useful members of their family, society, and community. Or, to speak generally, they will become useful members of humanity. This is the practical meaning of Zen.

Second, Zen is "spiritual" because Zen does not "eat earthly meals but talk about heavenly matters". On the contrary, Zen's approach is to "eat earthly meals and also talk about earthly matters". This is the practical spirituality that the Buddha upheld during his 45 years teaching the dhamma. He did not hold up mirages in front of people but taught them to use their sensory organs *to see and know things as they are,* or to stimulate the ultimate faculties of the Wordless Awareness Mind. At a higher level, he also taught people to use their cognitive awareness to come face to face with the true reality, which is Suchness (Tathatā).

Through the fundamental practice methods that I mentioned above, Zen helps us exploit our latent spiritual energy. This is the energy that provides us with creativity, innovation, natural eloquence, and radiates as *compassion, loving-kindness, equanimity and sympathetic joy*. This energy is the only hope that humans have to avoid becoming a cog in the gigantic and frenetic machine called "human activity". We will be able to experience what it means to be a "witness". We will also be able to experience the support that spirituality gives us in our worldly and spiritual lives.

2. *Harmony as a focal point*

Zen does not want us to disengage from our current life. On the contrary, it wants us to engage with life to create harmonious situations in the individual, family, society, community, and natural environment. Our life before we follow the Zen path contains many disharmonies. We experience disharmony in our body and internal organs, in our mental and physiological well-being, in our family, work place, and community life. We all have experienced, to various extents, this state of disharmony. Once we have entered the Zen path, studied and practiced its teaching, we will experience harmony in our body and mind, then within our family and circle of friends. Our life will become more meaningful: we do not run away from our responsibilities toward the environment that surrounds us.

For this reason, I place harmony as a focal point of Zen teaching. It is a practical need of the scientifically-minded and clear-headed Zen practitioner.

Sorrow and suffering will only dissipate when we experience harmony in our body and mind. Only then will the seeds of conflict, dispute, aggression, envy, jealousy, calumny, and hatred be extinguished in the darker parts of our mind. Our life will become truly useful to our family, society, and humanity.

On these fundamental foundations, security and order, as well as prosperity and growth within the community, society, and religious community, can be effectively and actively built. If each individual within a family, community, organization, or religion has harmony within their body and mind, this family, community, organization, or religion will experience true peace, happiness, harmony, prosperity, and altruism. When this condition is not met, this family, organization, or religion will be in a state of permanent unease; parents, children, husbands, wives, and in-laws will rarely live happily and harmoniously; employees of the organization will continuously be in strife, leading to strikes and violence; the religion will always experience struggle and contention leading to bloodshed, atrocious killing, and self-harm.

For these reasons, harmony is the focal point of Zen. Without it, each environment will experience trouble, disturbance, and latent competition, conflict, contention, and aggression, even though the environment may be a

A SPIRITUAL SCIENCE 89

solemn place of worship such as a temple, pagoda, small temple, or holy place.

This is why I never mention in my teaching that the aim of practicing Zen is to become a Buddha, an Arahat, or a Bodhisattva, or to attain freedom from concern and liberation, but always focus on harmony.

3. What constitutes harmony

Harmony is a realistic goal that the Zen practitioner should aim for. It is the foundation on which spiritual wisdom develops. It is also the first marker on the spiritual path. In order to travel deeper along the spiritual path, the Zen practitioner must first experience harmony, or at least a small part of it. Harmony consists first of harmony within the body and within the mind, and eventually between body and mind. In the case of the Buddha, before he started his teaching period, he had spent time attaining harmony in his body and mind and developing his spiritual wisdom. Although we cannot aspire to match the Buddha's attainments, we need to at least understand the essence of harmony in order to see clearly our direction of travel.

Regarding the body

Our body consists of many parts such as our internal organs, sensory organs, circulatory system, nervous system, and limbs. Illness occurs when these parts are not in harmony with each other. If we apply the Buddha's teaching in the suttas and the Buddhist Patriarchs' teaching in the commentaries through Zen's practical exercises and meditation techniques, we will be able to alleviate the disturbances in our internal organs and limbs. This is achieved by resolving the hormonal imbalances in our endocrine system through the methods of samatha (tranquility), samādhi (stillness of mind), paññā (wisdom) and anupassanā (contemplation), which leads to harmony within our body.

The teaching plays a very important role. It is the teaching, applied by the mind, which impacts on the brain, endocrine glands, and autonomic nervous system. However, if the mind is dull-witted, even the sublime teaching of the Buddha would not be able to save the body. For the teaching needs to be applied by an *awakened mind* or an *awakened Intellect* to reach its full and harmonious achievement. A strong determination, but combined with a dull-witted and undiscerning mind, will not lead to any alleviation of illnesses of the body. The determining condition is the correct teaching put into practice by an awakened mind or awakened Intellect. A strong determination can lead to a body in ruin, as the Buddha experienced when he pursued extreme self-mortification for nearly six years. His mind at the time was still deluded as he blindly trusted the self-mortification practice.

We should never rely on the power of the mind, but instead on its awakening and clear-headedness, in order to apply the correct teaching and correct technique to activate in our practice the parasympathetic nervous system, functions of the Wordless Awareness Mind, or higher still the Tathā-Mind.

Regarding the mind

Our mind consists of many groups. When we use the five aggregates model, we talk about Form, Feelings and Sensations, Perception, Mental Formations and Consciousness. When we use the three aspects of mind model, we talk about Thinking Faculty, Consciousness and Intellect. When these groups do not act in harmony with each other, we have a volatile character, constantly switching between: love, dislike, joy, and sadness; welcoming and distant; tenseness and lethargy; friendship and enmity; from close allies to implacable enemies. This is because inside these groups lie hidden the energy of mental defilements/old habits, fetters, underlying tendencies, and karmic hindrances. As we apply and assiduously practice the Zen teaching passed down by the Buddha and Buddhist Patriarchs, we have the capacity to bring these groups into harmony with each other. We will then experience joy, serenity, and altruism; our body is healthy, we feel full of energy and our steps are graceful.

The important factor

We need to experience for ourselves the harmony within ourselves, with harmony of mind being the most important factor. When the various functions within our mind are in harmony, we will experience a feeling of tranquility, purity, joy, composure, and calmness. We do not get attached and do not carry subjective prejudices and fixed opinions about others. We do not persist with unrealistic dreams and ambitions. We are free from thoughts of envy, hatred, tyranny, and cruelty toward others. Our internal organs will be in harmonious balance, especially our liver and kidneys. When our emotions arise, they impact first on our liver and kidneys and then on our heart, stomach, and intestines. When we feel anger, irritation, or resentment, our liver is impacted. When we feel anxiety or fear, our kidneys are impacted. Biochemicals such as norepinephrine, epinephrine, and cortisol are secreted in response to these emotional states.

I have often said: "Love, compassion, loving-kindness, free-spiritedness, generosity, tolerance, forgiveness, and serenity are all founded upon the energy of harmony". Consequently, morality and good citizenship are also founded upon the energy of harmony. As an example, the Buddhist four immeasurable qualities of *compassion, loving-kindness, sympathetic joy* and *equanimity* do not occur naturally. This is why I have chosen harmony as a focal point for an appropriate practice, meaning that all spiritual practices need to have harmony as their central point. I did not choose enlightenment, liberation, attaining Buddha-hood or attaining Arahat-hood as the focal point. These lofty ideals are certainly worthy; however in the context of our times, I consider them to be unrealistic. Our mind will never be at peace if we keep mulling over these distant dreams.

I often give this example:

"Anyone can dream whatever dream they like, but when you have entered Zen practice, you should put these dreams into a drawer and lock them up. Do not think about these dreams any more. Only in this way can you practice Zen. If you fail to do so, the verbal chatter in the mind and the building up of false thoughts will never cease. You will never be able to vanquish false thoughts. It is because your dreams, lofty as they may be, are false thoughts."

Many Zen practitioners fail to recognize this minor mistake, and as a result cannot silence their false thoughts after many years of practice. Their false thoughts continue to lead them on a wandering path. They keep talking about "letting go of false thoughts" but their Intellect keeps drawing ever new ones. As a result, their body and mind are never in harmony.

4. Meaning of harmony

In a psychological sense, harmony means "not in contradiction" or "not in opposition". It also means that all elements that are associated within a time period or in the same environment accord with each other.

Example No 1:

Flowering plants, trees and ponds within the grounds of the monastery are planted and set up in good proportion to each other. A visitor will find them pleasing to the eye. We can say that the grounds of the monastery have harmony.

By contrast, if plants are not well looked after and are not sufficiently watered to withstand the dry weather and are dying or stunted, if weeds are growing everywhere and are not cleared out, we can say that the grounds of the monastery do not have harmony.

Example No 2:

The meditation class has a prefect who is assigned the task of time keeper, reminding Master of times for breaks, and ringing the bell to wake fellow students up in the morning for Qi Gong practice, etc. Meditation students hear the bell and know what the next activity is; their role is to wake up promptly and attend the Qi Gong session, not lingering a few more minutes in bed. The study support group knows that their task is to serve meals, wash the dishes, and keep the dining room and class room tidy without needing any reminder. Everyone goes about their tasks joyfully and responsibly without raising any complaint. This is the image of harmony in an organization, using the meditation class as an example.

In summary, the cause for this harmony lies in fostering a spirit of taking responsibility and serving others. Assigning tasks without also promoting the spirit of responsibility will only lead to disharmony within the group.

Harmony within a living organism occurs when the functions of internal organs are all in balance. When each is in balance, all are in balance. When one is disturbed, the others will be affected.

We can say generally that harmony is founded upon the accord of factors or psychological states of individuals within a group such as the family, meditation class, or organization. No-one is in opposition to others in their daily activities. Everyone is happy with each other and enjoys peaceful association and amity. Finally, everyone understands that they have a responsibility and duty toward others.

5. *Making harmony real*

In order to make harmony a reality within the individual, Zen has designed many practical exercises and meditation techniques to guide the practice of the teaching of the Buddha and Buddhist Patriarchs in everyday life. These practice instruments have the effect of creating an effective psychological and physiological feedback loop that helps the practitioner develop a new perspective based on mutual assistance and the absence of reasoning, labeling, and slandering each other. Examples are: knowledge of the Three Characteristics of Worldly Phenomena and the Law of Cause and Effect; or practicing Just Knowing, Knowing-things-as-they-are, Non-verbal Knowing, and Silent Awareness.

Under the psychological feedback loop, we start with transforming our old perspective of life into a new perspective. With our old perspective, our mind is often attached to things, affected by vanity and superiority, equality, or inferiority complexes. All of these originate from a subjective perspective. With this perspective, our mind can never achieve harmony within itself. It can never stand still, stay pure or be content with what it has. It is like a donkey chasing the carrot that dangles in front of it, or a monkey ceaselessly jumping from one branch to another. On that basis, we will never be content with what we have. We will never get the opportunity to live with joy, serenity, and lightness toward other people and the environment. Our mind is always agitated.

With our new perspective, we start to recognize that the true characteristics of worldly phenomena are impermanence, conflict, and insubstantiality. Human nature is constantly influenced by these three characteristics. We will feel less sorrow and suffering when things come into our grasp and then vanish from it. Yesterday we were a wealthy person, today we are bankrupt. Yesterday we had a job, today we are retrenched. Yesterday we had all our close relatives, today some of them are buried by a storm, or an earthquake. We now know that this reflects the laws of impermanence, conflict, and absence of real substance in action within the phenomenal world.

When we study and practice the Buddha's teaching, we gain psychological feedback. We become awakened. We have a new perspective. With this new perspective, our mind is stable, serene, and devoid of attachments. Physiological feedback will also occur inside our body. This action and response principle helps us alleviate or terminate our psychosomatic illnesses.

Nowadays, when we study Zen, we need to clearly understand these feedback concepts. This is the law of cause and effect in action. A correct action leads to a favorable result. An incorrect action leads to an unfavorable one. We do not blame karma as those who lack confidence often do.

Understanding the physiological feedback loop in Zen helps us understand the principle of action and effect when we practice the topics that the Buddha taught. Harmony is built upon the basis of this feedback loop.

We will not fear that we may be practicing incorrectly when we understand the scientific reasons that underlie the physiological feedback loop in Zen.

6. *Zen is not passive*

Zen does not teach us to run away from life, but on the contrary, to engage with life. Zen does not encourage people to abandon their responsibilities toward family and society in order to attain some faraway phantasmagoric state. On the contrary, Zen encourages people to fulfill their current responsibilities and duties when they do not yet have the strength to let go of all worldly and religious matters.

Zen can help us better fulfill these current duties and responsibilities if we realize that it really does have the capacity to help us attain goals that are relevant to various stages of our life journey.

For example, if our body has a chronic illness such as high blood pressure, insomnia, asthma, or stomach ulcers, Zen will teach us to practice the methods of anupassanā (contemplation), samatha (tranquility), samādhi (stillness of mind) and paññā (wisdom) to make our body healthy. We may choose to apply the method that fits our capacity the most. Zen does not teach us to say prayers, chant mantras, or recite suttas to get our body back to health. Neither does Zen encourage us to "sit and hold onto these illnesses, consider them as friends, until they reach their highest development". Zen does not hold such passive approaches.

7. *Spiritual energy*

Through being conceptualized as a spiritual science, Zen has clearly shown us that we have within ourselves the energies that can make our body healthy and our mind joyful and serene, bring harmony to our mind and body, and develop our creative insights and wisdom. These energies have always been latent in the hundreds of billions of brain cells, and in areas of the cerebral cortex, endocrine system, and autonomic nervous system. If we know how to apply the methods that Zen prescribes, we will be able to exploit these energies to alleviate by ourselves illnesses of our body and mind, and recover our memory. Higher still, we will be able to exploit the potential for enlightenment that is innate to our brain.

We will be able to recognize that changing our karma, freedom from suffering, enlightenment and liberation from birth and death, and the witness principle are all founded on the spiritual energy in Zen.

8. *What is spirituality?*

The spiritual mind is beyond the worldly mind and the religious mind. It is devoid of impurities that come from mental defilements/old habits, fetters and underlying tendencies. It is absolutely pure. The Buddha called it the "clear-water pond". It originates from our Wordless

Awareness Mind. It has creativity as its character, and carries the latent energies of compassion, loving-kindness, and enlightened wisdom, which are Buddha-nature. Unlike the worldly mind and religious minds, it does not have the self as subject but consists of the Wordless Awareness Mind and, at a higher level, Buddha-nature. Developmental Buddhism gave it a fictitious title called "True Self" or "The Pure and Tranquil Ego". Zen Buddhism gave it a fictitious title called "The Master".

In the spiritual mind, unlike the worldly or religious minds, there is no conflict and perverted struggle; no yearning for material or spiritual interests that lead to conflicts, enmities, and vicious plots to bring down, kill, or purge other people; no praying to deities, blind faith, or superstition; no trampling on people to gain an advantage; no personality cult, clique, and discrimination based on rank or class; no craving, ambition, selfishness, and individualism; and no subjective prejudice, fixed opinion, and bias. Finally, the spiritual mind does not lead to wars like the worldly or religious minds, but to harmony, amity, friendliness, love, constructiveness, and service.

While the spiritual mind is founded upon our Wordless Awareness Mind and Buddha-nature, the worldly or religious minds are founded upon the Thinking Faculty, Consciousness and Intellect. These three aspects of the human mind lead people to little peace but much sorrow, suffering, sadness, and hatred; little tolerance, forgiveness, generosity, and sympathy but much terror, harsh punishment, retribution, purging, and intransigence; little relying on each other to grow and much trampling on others to live; little awakening and much delusion and clinging; little compassion, loving-kindness, sympathetic joy, and equanimity and much labeling and slander; little sincerity and much duplicity and treachery; little honesty and much fabrication and pretense.

9. *Objectives*

Through one of the four means of anupassanā (contemplation), samatha (tranquility), samādhi (stillness of mind) and paññā (wisdom), Zen aims at guiding the practitioner into using practical exercises and meditation techniques to achieve the following effects:

❖ First, stimulate the endocrine glands to help alleviate and end psychosomatic illnesses and bring changes to the human character such as:

The serotonergic system in the pineal gland and brain stem. Serotonin has the following properties:

- Regulate the sleep-wake cycle; alleviate anxiety, nervous breakdown, and stress.
- Increase energy level and enthusiasm for work.
- Increase patience, not giving in to despondency.

The melatonin system in the pineal gland, the paraventricular nuclei of the hypothalamus, and the brain stem. Melatonin has the following properties:

- Treat chronic insomnia (re-adjust the sleep-wake cycle).
- Prevent chest cancer and brain tumors.
- Decrease blood pressure; regulate the cardio-vascular system.

- Prevent strokes.
- Prevent heart attacks.
- Control skin pigmentations and prevent harmful effects of toxins in the blood.
- Treat cataracts.
- Recover memory.
- Stimulate the immune system.

The acetylcholine system in the brain stem and at nerve endings of the parasympathetic system. Acetylcholine has the following properties:

- Alleviate high blood pressure, high blood cholesterol.
- Alleviate memory impairment.
- Help sharpen the intellect and increase alertness.
- Strengthen the cardio-vascular system.
- Counterbalance the effect of norepinephrine and epinephrine.

The Dopamine system in the brain stem. Dopamine triggers the feeling of elation and bliss in meditation. It also helps alleviate Parkinson's disease and schizophrenia. The latter manifests as hallucinations caused by an excess of glutamate and a lack of dopamine in the two occipital and temporal lobes that impairs the hearing and seeing functions.

- ❖ Second, maintain hormonal homeostasis in the body in general, and in the internal organs in particular.

- ❖ Third, exploit the creative energy of the Wordless Awareness Mind: Ultimate Seeing, Ultimate Hearing, Ultimate Touch and Ultimate Cognitive Awareness which corresponds to Buddha-nature. These creative energies constitute the spiritual energy in Zen that is developed through the process of truth realization or spiritual realization.

  When biochemical substances that are beneficial to the body are secreted, we will experience harmony within body and mind, or a state of hormonal homeostasis in the body.

  Finally, when spiritual energy is exploited from the ultimate faculties of our Wordless Awareness Mind and Buddha-nature, we will experience more clearly the value of Zen to human life.

- ❖ We will experience a truly joyful and serene life for our body and mind are truly in harmony:

  - Our body is healthy as our internal organs, and most importantly our liver and kidneys, have reached hormonal homeostasis.

  - Our mind goes from being full of attachments, to fewer attachments, and finally no attachment. Or, when we are aware of an attachment, we know how to gently stop the attachment at its source.

- ❖ We no longer hold feelings of envy, vilification, labeling, slander, and complaint toward people around us. We will lose the bad habits of furtively defaming people who are not present. We will prefer to find our own little faults in order to correct them, rather than finding faults in others in order to judge them.

❖ Our mind or nervous system is no longer stressed by dissatisfactions that always occur in life. Or, when stress arises, we can stop it immediately by using one of Zen's breathing methods.

❖ Our mind is no longer disturbed, aimlessly agitated, and attached. Our anxieties and fears fade away. Our subjective prejudices, fixed opinions, and biases progressively diminish. We often dwell in Full and Clear Awareness.

❖ Our body no longer carries chronic illnesses such as insomnia, diabetes, asthma, and allergies. We have the capacity to prevent cancer and cure genetic diseases.

❖ Our spiritual wisdom gradually develops as we practice the topics of anupassanā (contemplation), samatha (tranquility), samādhi (stillness of mind) and paññā (wisdom).

❖ Finally, we will have the ability to better serve our family and society:

- We are not addicted to drugs, gambling, and debauchery; involved in gangs; working in dishonest occupations; neglecting our family; having blind faith and believing in superstitions.

- We have a high sense of self-sufficiency, neither pessimistic nor optimistic. We are always joyful because our stillness of mind (samādhi) and wisdom (paññā) have developed.

- We do not abandon our responsibilities and duties within our family, work place, or association. When our spiritual wisdom has opened up, our physical constitution becomes stronger due to the hormonal homeostasis in our body and internal organs, our sense of responsibility will automatically grow.

- Our spirit is not debased. We do not give in to superstitions, pessimism, and misanthropy, or wait for death to arrive while we still have strength and energy to work.

- We have totally changed our perspective on life. We have confidence in the teaching of the Buddha because we have experienced true elation and bliss through the practice of anupassanā (contemplation), samatha (tranquility), samādhi (stillness of mind) and paññā (wisdom).

10. A shining example

For those of us who are adults, through the Zen practices that I mentioned above, we will become a shining example to our children. We no longer need to fear that our children will turn bad, become rebellious, join a street gang, or run away from home; or become obdurate, stupid, or slow-witted; or become a threat to society and social order. For, through our Zen practice, we will have created one of three types of energy:

First is the energy of harmony.

We are not irritable, hard to please, complaining, distorting the truth, and harsh when we interact with our children. As we express the qualities of compassion and loving-kindness toward our children, we are able to touch them. They will willingly listen to what we say and become well-behaved, respectful of elders, socially responsible, self-sufficient, and persevering.

Second is the energy of example.

Through our daily activities such as sitting in meditation at set times of the day, attending monthly practice community meetings, or attending meditation retreats, and through the manner in which we interact with members of our family and colleagues at work, we will exert a good influence on our children. When our children reach the age of understanding (from seven years up), they will be able to imitate us and sit in meditation, or ask us to explain the practical benefits of practicing Zen. We will be able to set a good example for our children and influence them for the better. In the future, we will not need to fear that the seeds of enlightenment may become stunted. For when the causal conditions for our current life have ended, our children may continue to follow the path of practical spiritual practice that the Buddha has passed on to us.

Third is the energy field created by compassion.

When we have practiced over a long period of time and experienced deep states of samādhi, we will experience the energy field created by compassion. This energy field will have a good influence on our children. We will not need to fear that the seed of enlightenment will die in our family when we leave this world. Our children will follow our example and practice Zen with the aim of developing their spiritual energy.

Fourth is the transformation of our genes.

When a Zen practitioner experiences deep samādhi, they have the ability to create new nuclei from inside the nucleus and nucleolus of their neurons by transforming the nucleus and nucleolus of each neuron. This is because the nucleus and nucleolus are activated when we manage to stop thoughts in a stable manner. During this process, the subtle mental defilements/old habits that lie latent in the DNA (deoxyribonucleic acid) and RNA (ribonucleic acid), which are the deepest part of the nucleus and nucleolus respectively, of each neuron are expelled and eliminated. Furthermore we also have the ability to self-treat genetic disorders, or illnesses that we have carried for a very long time but could not cure. Genetic materials are stored in the DNA inside the nucleus and RNA inside the nucleolus of each neuron.

You will need to progress to the Wisdom Meditation classes to experience deep samādhi states through meditating on abstract topics such as Emptiness and Suchness. In contrast, at the level of the Fundamental Meditation class you will only have the ability to stop your thinking for a little while, for example by practicing the Just Knowing topic.

I often use simple colloquial language to make Zen easier to understand and say that we need to "tighten the nuts and bolts" of our decrepit car. Our car is now very old. It is creaking everywhere and is not as solid as when it was newer. Therefore we need to use pliers to tighten these nuts and bolts. Our pliers here are our samādhi practice.

Through the samādhi method, we activate our neurons to treat illnesses and eliminate the subtle mental defilements/old habits.

The principle for karma transformation and being a witness in Zen lies in the samādhi method. Through samādhi, we will transform our neurons by changing the DNA and RNA inside them.

11. Actively contributing

Through being a good example, as mentioned above, we have contributed our abilities in building security and order in society. This contribution consists of the spirit of altruism, compassion, knowledge, and wisdom, and also because our children have become serving and constructive members of their families and society.

Wherever our children live, there is harmony and a spirit of service. The spirit of altruism will always be present, compassion, knowledge, and wisdom will constantly be developed, for they have learnt the spiritual tradition passed on by the Buddha through living with us from birth to adulthood.

This shows that good citizenship does not rely solely on the national education system but is founded upon the traditions followed within the family, in particular how parents conduct themselves. We need to pay particular attention to the genes that are passed on by parents.

Our brain and physical constitution is the result of an evolutionary process that goes back millions of years. A person who has been impregnated with the Zen spirit in all four postures through practicing according to the teaching of the Buddha has *new* genes.

The key to enlightenment and liberation from birth and death

In order to experience spiritual development, we need to realize the concept of *tathā*. This is the key to experiencing spiritual development in Zen. The concept of *tathā* is at the origin of the enlightenment of the Buddha. Later, this concept was developed by Developmental Buddhist masters into what is "beyond speech", "beyond thought", and "beyond comprehension".

I consider *tathā* and *tathatā* as the catalysts that trigger our potential for enlightenment. I will explain and guide the practice on this matter at a later stage.

Consequences of the long past

Before following the Zen path, most of us would have spent nearly or over a half century pursuing worldly pleasures. Anxiety, fear, terror, suffering, and sorrow would have also been present in no small measure. However all of us have relied on our body to enjoy pleasures according to our opportunities and capabilities. When we live in the world, we all play a role within our circle of life and we all pursue pleasures and indulge. Enjoying food and drink, competing, and disputing were common refrains in our daily worldly life.

Previously, we were probably not really awakened, and our senses were still attached to the tastes of pleasure, fame, status, and various interests. Our mental defilements/old habits had the opportunity to accumulate more sensual pleasures and emotions in pursuit of fame and prosperity. Our Intellect had to continuously face thorny problems needing to be solved in our daily life or in the positions that we occupied. We had to face and deal with difficult, terrifying, and distressing situations that generated a high level of stress. When our emotions ran high, biochemicals were released in high doses in our sympathetic nervous system and endocrine system in accordance with the emotional stress. When our nervous system was constantly under stress, we found it difficult to avoid psychosomatic illnesses such as high blood pressure, irregular heartbeat, stomach ulcers, diabetes, and chronic insomnia. These were the consequences from our long past.

We have now awakened, committed ourselves to the Zen path and decided to live the monastic life at the monastery like the monks and nuns for three months, or a month or several weeks as some of you have done. However, how can your body go back to 100% normalcy in such a short period of time? We cannot use samādhi (stillness of mind) or paññā (wisdom) methods to cure in a day the chronic illnesses that our body has been carrying for a long time.

The profound cause is that self-generated transcendental wisdom has not emerged within us through the Wisdom level meditation topics that we have been practicing. Most fundamentally, we have not completely transformed our old perspective on life. As a result, our mind has not concluded the conflict within itself. Furthermore, we have not yet experienced deep samādhi states. When we sit in meditation, inner talk and inner dialogue still arise at times or continuously.

In this situation, we find it difficult to alleviate the illnesses that we carry in our body. It is only natural that our internal organs, circulatory system, and inner energy cannot yet reach a state of balance. This is the result of the long worldly life that we have led in the past. We have endured life for too long. For some of us, it is a half century, or nearly a century, or more than 40 years. We have now awakened and decided to return to the Dhamma. Our mind has changed somewhat but our body still carries many chronic illnesses. This is the consequence of the long period in which our body and mind were immersed in worldly pleasures.

Our body and mind need harmony

Our body is now like an old car. From the outside, it looks healthy, but inside nuts and bolts are all loose and creaking. Our joints no longer link tightly with our muscles and nerves. Our internal organs no longer work like they did when we were young. We are all affected by one illness or another. Now that you practice Zen with the purpose of maintaining a healthy body, you will need to combine your practice with Qi Gong breathing, healthy eating, and taking herbal supplements to readjust your cardio vascular system and internal organs, and strengthen your immune system. Only when your body is healthy can your mind find peace to continue to practice. If your body is beset by illnesses, you will lose your enthusiasm for practice. This is the principle of mutual interaction between body and mind. Body and mind need to be both in harmony. This harmony is also the fundamental outcome of spiritual practice using the Zen method. Body and mind, mind and body need to be in harmony with each other. If they are not in harmony, our practice will be impeded. You need to pay attention to this point.

Protecting the body, transforming the mind

Not until we have practiced to the point where we are *totally in control of our thinking*, or experience *wordless cognitive awareness in a stable manner*, can we be no longer concerned with protecting our body. The body will then be healthy by itself. Our psychosomatic illnesses are gradually eliminated. We will then practice sitting meditation to develop our spiritual energy by using our wordless cognitive awareness and inserting a practice topic into it. Mental defilements/old habits are eliminated and psychosomatic illnesses will cure themselves. The reason is the components of the axis Wordless Awareness Mind - hypothalamus - parasympathetic nervous system - brain stem - endocrine system interact with each other to secrete biochemical substances that are beneficial to our body such as dopamine, acetylcholine, serotonin, melatonin, and insulin.

When we have not yet reached this stage, we need to protect our body by adding Qi Gong to our practice. We practice breathing to regulate our inner energy and blood flows and generate or strengthen our immune system to help keep our body healthy and alleviate prior illnesses. A weak body not only does not provide us with the energy necessary for a sustained spiritual practice or altruistic work, it also adversely impacts on the enthusiasm, diligence, and perseverance of the mind. A tired body leads to a mind that is easily discouraged, irritated, and regressing. I consider that we should use Qi Gong to support the practice of Zen in the early stages. Once we have really experienced samādhi in a stable manner, changed our perspective on life and awakened our Intellect, we will no longer need the support of Qi Gong breathing.

At this point of our Zen journey, our body is the only instrument that can help us complete the journey. If the body is half-paralyzed or needs to continuously lie in bed due to illness, we will never be able to practice Zen even if we have a very strong will and powerful mind. Our Zen practice will come to an impasse for our mind cannot be at

A SPIRITUAL SCIENCE 111

peace, and our body cannot sit, walk or stand to maintain our practice. We need to realize that, although the mind is the master, it is always influenced by the body! Only when the body is healthy can the mind be reassured, awake, and lucid to practice. Conversely, only when the mind is at peace can the body be comfortable when sitting in meditation. Body and mind, mind and body always maintain a mutual interaction. They both influence each other. The mind has the ability to generate illness or health in the body. On the other hand, the body has the ability to create obstacles for the mind as well as helping the mind feel comfort and tranquility when it is healthy. Fatigue and sleepiness are caused by a tired, weak body and lead to the mind lacking alertness when sitting in meditation.

Our direction

As a general rule, the ability for the Zen practitioner to reach their ultimate destination always relies on the principle of harmony between body and mind. This is the most fundamental principle. The teaching might be sublime, the techniques might be ingenious but without harmony between body and mind, our spiritual journey will still come to an impasse. When we set the direction for our journey, we need to see clearly this point: body and mind need to be in balance. The crucial elements are a healthy body and an awakened mind. If the mind is not awakened, sooner or later the body will develop illnesses. Conversely, if the body is not healthy, sooner or later the mind will be in tatters. Courage is a much required quality of the mind, however if the body is not healthy, the mind will not be able to materialize this courage over the long term. Conversely, if the body is healthy but the mind is not ready to engage on the Zen path, the body will not be able to maintain its good health over the long term. The body is like the fuel, the mind is like the light. The light given by the lamp needs the fuel. Once the fuel is exhausted, the light is extinguished. And the death-consciousness would leave the body!

Initially, we need to aim at protecting the body and restoring its health. We can consider that the mind has tentatively a new direction. The Intellect has been awakened, and we have started to leave behind worldly matters and resolved to follow the spiritual path.

For those of you who have committed to become a Buddhist monk or nun, your directions are freedom from suffering, enlightenment, and liberation from birth and death. This is a positive and tangible objective. However, to make it concrete, you will need to study and practice the topics that are appropriate for your objective. As the most immediate necessary condition, you need to recover or protect the health of your body. As second necessary condition, you need to concretize the fundamental teaching in your daily life at the monastery. Your demeanor and conduct need to adequately reflect your position as student monk or nun. You need to adhere to the protocols that have been laid out in the rules and regulations of the monastery. There is an appropriate time for each activity. The third necessary condition is to clearly understand the teaching and practice. You need to understand the teaching to change your life perspective, and you need to understand the practice to apply it to its full completion. At the Wisdom level, the cognition map is the key instrument that will help you achieve your objectives of freedom from suffering, enlightenment, and liberation from birth and death. Without this instrument, you will find it difficult to reach your destination.

As for the lay Buddhist practitioner, you need not think about liberation from birth and death and should focus on reducing suffering and developing your insight and wisdom. For lay practitioners, most of the suffering comes from chronic illnesses of the body and unending disturbance in the mind. Therefore the fundamental objective for lay practitioners is a healthy body and peaceful mind. Attaining spiritual enlightenment is an added bonus, but liberation from birth and death should be considered out of reach. Unlike monks and nuns, lay practitioners do not have sufficient conditions to seek liberation from birth and death and will find it very difficult to imitate monks and nuns. You will need to cut all worldly relationships and worldly knowledge and practice with vigor and assiduity. Therefore lay practitioners should aim at achieving a healthy body, peaceful mind, and some spiritual experience through Wisdom level practices. This is because you still have too many attachments to your family and society. You cannot sever the feelings of love toward your children or your grandchildren. Some of you have young children or grandchildren who need your protection as their parents or grandparents. Some of you need to work to repay housing loans or car loans and pay health insurance. Some of you are caught up in the give and take involved in social relationships. This is why lay practitioners cannot sever abruptly all worldly relationships and worldly knowledge like monks and nuns. However, if you wish to engage in a focused practice like monks and nuns, you can. You can become a full time vegetarian and practice sitting meditation regularly at home at set times of the day. You can restrain yourself from indulgences; limit your social interactions, dinner parties, public gatherings, and festivities; gradually forgo spectacles, travel, and sightseeing as well as books, magazines, radio, and television. Only in this way can you avoid adding to the store of mental defilements/old habits in your mind. Only then can you have the chance to vanquish the desires of the egoistic self. Only then can your spiritual practice bear fruit.

You should set up a dedicated room in your house where you practice topics covered in the Fundamental Meditation class or in Wisdom Intermediate Level classes such as: As-it-is, the Four Noble Truths, No-self, Law of Co-dependent Arising, Law of Dependently Arisen Phenomena, Emptiness, Suchness, and Illusion, etc. In addition, you may set aside every month one or two days during weekends to participate in a retreat at your practice community or at the monastery.

Only by doing these measures would you concretize your spiritual environment and make your direction tangible. Otherwise you will find it difficult to be successful on the Zen path.

Role of the body

I would like to take this opportunity to remind you that our spirit of study and practice is the Bodhisattva spirit. A healthy body is the only means that can help the mind achieve good conditions of practice. It is also the vehicle that leads the mind to freedom from suffering, enlightenment, and liberation from birth and death. Finally it is the means by which the mind can help others. If the body collapses, we will not be able to sit in meditation even though the mind may be determined to practice assiduously. The mind may make great vows, such as terminate all sorrow, follow the Bodhisattva path for life after life ever after and help all beings, etc., but without a healthy body we will not be able to realize any part of these great vows. For these reasons, if you want to reach your ultimate destination or to experience what Zen teaches, do not underestimate the role of the body. It is the vehicle that takes us to our destination. It is the boat that helps the mind cross the sea of birth and death. Whether we are able to realize our great vows depends largely on a healthy body and a peaceful mind.

Cravings must be vanquished

If we think that we can eat and drink to satisfy our senses come what may, we are not being clear-headed! Or rather, we are being driven by our mental defilements/old habits. A person who travels on the spiritual path must realize this point. We take food to provide fuel for our boat-body so that it runs smoothly and durably, and eventually takes us to the other shore, which is the place of ultimate liberation. We do not use eating and drinking as a means to satisfy our senses. The more our senses are satisfied, the more mental defilements get accumulated in our mind. Passions and addictions are built upon these pleasures and satisfactions.

Some people say: "When we drink alcohol, we just see it as it is! Let's not call it alcohol. We can drink alcohol as if it is water!"

How high is our addiction level if we consider alcohol just like water? And how bad is the impact on our nervous system and stomach? If you consider that you can drink alcohol as if it is water, your karma will never get transformed and you can never use Zen to take you to your ultimate spiritual destination. You must know how to vanquish your craving for food and drink. You must recognize that food and drink are medicines that can keep the body healthy so that the mind can be at peace and concentrate on the spiritual practice.

When our body is ill, we may need to follow a diet. This is the right thing to do. But we are in the wrong if we follow extreme diets. This is a case of form taking over character. We need to place the right focus and have a new perspective and new direction on eating. This perspective consists of seeing the body as a means that the mind can use for its spiritual practice and then to save other beings. If we wish to follow the Bodhisattva path but our body is constantly ill and our mind constantly attached to things, how can we attain samādhi (stillness of mind) and paññā (wisdom) and the skillful means that will help us save other beings? This is why we need to vanquish the craving for food and drink while eschewing either extreme diets or careless eating. We need to have a scientific approach to eating.

We need to change our perspective on eating.

The body is very precious

In order to attain freedom from suffering, enlightenment, and ultimate liberation from birth and death, we need our body and our brain for our spiritual practice. The Buddha, before he attained Buddha-hood, had to rely on his body made of the four elements to practice. The same applies to all Buddhist Patriarchs. This is why we should not underestimate the role of the body.

It is truly an instrument that we need to use. We need its help if we wish to successfully cross the sea of birth and death, or develop our spiritual wisdom. If the body is ill, we will not be able to practice even though the mind wants to practice assiduously. On the contrary, the more the body is ill the more the mind is affected by those illnesses of the body. Therefore, the body is very precious, but if we consider it as a means to satisfy our craving for worldly pleasures, it will become the cause for endless birth and death.

When the Buddha expounded on the truth of Suffering in his teaching on the Four Noble Truths, he listed as the 13th suffering the attachment to our body made of the five aggregates and believing it to be real. From this belief arise the concepts of "I", "mine", "I am", "I should be", "I will be". Belief in the reality of the self, love of the self, clinging to the reality of the self, and seeking sensual pleasures for the self will follow.

Save oneself, save others

With our new perspective, we need to see the body as the only means that can help us practice and give us the opportunity to complete the Bodhisattva path. This path consists of *first save ourselves*, and *then save others*. If we have not had any experience of the spiritual path or have only limited experience through the Fundamental Meditation class, we should not step forward and guide others spiritually. By this restraint, we manifest the dual spirits of *compassion* and *knowledge* that both apply on the Bodhisattva path. We need to have a healthy body in order to be able to focus on our study and practice. We need to train our body and mind first to experience, albeit in limited fashion, the teaching of the Buddha and Buddhist Patriarchs. In this way, we will have equipped ourselves with the necessary baggage, even though this may consist only of basic elements of Zen. If we have not had any experience of Zen practice but still step forward to guide others, we will have failed the spirit of compassion and knowledge of the Bodhisattva path. Having compassion toward others is right. However we need to have knowledge to concretize this compassion because knowledge is the essential element for doing so. Compassion without knowledge is merely pitying others without having any means to help them overcome suffering and sorrow, and is therefore not realistic. It is not the compassion spirit of the Bodhisattva path. If we wish to save others by using some facets of Zen teaching, we need to have some experience of Zen practice. We need to experience it ourselves in order to be able to teach others with clarity. If we have not had the experience, we will feel bewildered or resort to generic answers when people ask us about specific difficulties that they encounter in their practice.

In our meditation practice, we need to be familiar with the way to get in and get out of each practice step. In this way, when we guide others we will not make mistakes because we have ourselves experienced each step. We know what is a correct practice and what is an incorrect one; we know when we have reached our goal and when we are treading water; we know what is oppressing body and mind, and what is relaxing mind and thoughts. These steps have already been committed into our own cognition map. We understand them clearly and completely because they have been committed to our memory and we have experienced them in our own body and mind. In this way, the Zen practice theory that we teach others comes from our own experience and is not made of some kind of reasoning and guessing. With our own inner experience, our helping others spirit will accord with the helping others spirit of the Bodhisattva path.

The important mutual interaction

There is another important matter in Zen practice that I would like to remind you of so that you will remember it well: when you practice Zen, your mind will always impact

A SPIRITUAL SCIENCE 119

on your brain. Under a correct impact, you will feel at ease and serene after a Zen practice session and if you take your blood pressure, you will see it stays the same or decreases. Under an incorrect impact, you will feel tired and heavy after a Zen practice session, and your blood pressure will increase.

This is why you need to be careful when you practice Zen. You may apply the Buddha's or Buddhist Patriarchs' teaching, but if you use an incorrect technique, the result may be illnesses or mental disturbances. This is because your mind always impacts on your brain when you practice Zen. If it impacts on the right areas, the body will be healthy and the mind peaceful and serene. But if it impacts on the wrong areas, the body will become ill, the mind disturbed and insights and wisdom will not develop. The mutual interaction between mind and brain is most important in Zen.

This interaction is the result of combined actions between five groups: teaching, mind, brain, endocrine glands, and biochemical substances.

Teaching is the teaching of the Buddha or Buddhist Patriarchs that has been transcribed in suttas and commentaries. Mind is the instrument for practice, i.e. we need to use our mind when we apply the teaching. This mind consists of the Thinking Faculty and the differentiating Consciousness. The Thinking Faculty performs the functions of thinking, pondering, reasoning, and judging, and includes the Intellect, language decoding areas and inner verbal chatter areas. The Consciousness operates by dualistic differentiation and includes the need to report.

As for the brain, relevant areas include the cerebral cortex, left hemisphere, right hemisphere, Wordless Awareness Mind areas, limbic system, brainstem, and biochemical substances.

When these various components interact with each other, biochemical substances will be released, resulting in a healthy or unhealthy body. I call this principle Zen's Biofeedback Mechanism.

Nowadays, with Zen seen as a spiritual science, it needs to establish its practice on very clear basis. This is why I have attempted to reconcile scientific discoveries about the brain with the teaching of the Buddha and Buddhist Patriarchs when we practice Zen.

I often say: "The West can explain and point to scientific evidence but does not know how to execute. The East can explain and execute, but is unable to point to scientific evidence." I am now attempting to use modern discoveries from neuroscience to demonstrate the validity of Zen's teaching from the East.

Difference between teaching the dhamma and teaching Zen practice

Furthermore, referring to science does not mean we do not recognize the illusory nature and illusory appearance of worldly phenomena. In reality, we do not use the Illusion doctrine to inhibit our or other people's mind, but recognize that people have not been able to free themselves from their old perspective as many layers of fetters or binding ties from worldly traditions still envelop their thinking. Therefore, we fully engage with the world in order to fulfill our vow of saving all beings in accordance with the Bodhisattva spirit. After having our own experience of Zen practice and our own realization of the essence of the Buddha's teaching through study and practice, we then guide others on the path. This guidance has value as it is realistic, concrete, and effective and widens the perspective of those who have not yet understood the teaching of the Buddha as captured in the suttas. It helps people really experience an alleviation of their body's illnesses, transformation of their mind's attachments and broadening of their spiritual wisdom.

This is the point of difference between a Zen teacher and a dhamma teacher. Teaching the dhamma relies on knowledge and education obtained through many years attending a school or university recognized by a diploma, bachelorship or doctorate in Buddhist studies which qualify the individual as a teacher. One has then the ability to become an erudite who has studied widely and retained suttas and commentaries well. Being a dhamma teacher does not require you to have your own experience in your body and mind, and how spiritual wisdom manifests itself, but requires you to have a good memory, innovation, and the ability to integrate suttas and commentaries from various schools of Buddhism, to present them and integrate into a system the remarkable points that one has learnt and discovered in the Buddha's and Buddhist Patriarchs' teaching in the suttas and commentaries. Being an erudite, or a scholar, or thesis writer relies on this principle.

In contrast, teaching Zen relies on your own experience of samādhi (stillness of mind) and self-generated paññā (wisdom). It requires you to "sample the taste of the dhamma" by yourself, whereas teaching the dhamma does not require you to sample its taste in your body, mind, and spiritual wisdom. Seeing the light of the path or having an inner experience of the path are based on this principle. A degree in Buddhist studies cannot validate the inner experience of a person who has seen the light of the path.

This is the clear difference between a dhamma teacher and a Zen teacher.

Self-reliance principle

Generally speaking, both samādhi (stillness of mind) and paññā (wisdom) cannot be obtained through attending a school, but can only be experienced by yourself through your own practice. Even the best teacher cannot help you experience them. Only you, by applying techniques taught by Zen, can experience them. This is why Zen promotes the *self-reliance principle*. Self-reliance means using your own energy to apply the practice topics taught by the Buddha in the suttas and by Buddhist Patriarchs in the commentaries. You cannot get help from anybody. You need to put in the effort to practice and then you will be able to experience samādhi or the alleviation of your psychosomatic illnesses. Just like when you were at school, if you want to succeed at the examination, you will need to master the content that you have learnt, and then use your own memory or intelligence to answer the questions asked at the examination. You cannot pray for the Buddha to help you pass the examination. Similarly, when you are ill, you need to buy the medications prescribed by your doctor and take them in accordance with your doctor's directions. You cannot use a charm or pray the Buddha to help you end your illness. This is the meaning of self-reliance in Zen.

Through many years of study and practice, we know how to concretize the Buddha's and Buddhist Patriarchs' teaching and shorten our practice.

Role of wordless cognitive awareness

When the egoistic self has become tranquil and pure, past karma will transform itself, the mind will transform itself, wisdom will develop by itself, and psychosomatic illnesses will alleviate themselves. This is the biofeedback principle in Zen. As long as the egoistic self is not yet tranquil and pure, the potential for enlightenment will not find the opportunity to spring forth. When the two pre-frontal cortex areas are continuously agitated, the speech formation and thought formation processes are permanently activated and the whole Wordless Awareness Mind cannot be present. You need to pay attention to this point.

If you assiduously practice the "No Talk" technique, you will be in firm control of your mental chatter, and inner talk and inner dialogue will both be under control. You will immediately have a clear cognitive awareness of the surrounding environment while your mental chatter is totally absent. This is the state of wordless cognitive awareness.

The concept of "Self" disappears and at that moment cognitive awareness is activated. The "I" and "Mine" concepts will continue to subsist until we experience wordless cognitive awareness, and the egoistic self cannot be absolutely tranquil and pure. Once we have experienced wordless cognitive awareness in a stable manner, we will immediately experience the absolutely tranquil and pure egoistic self.

I often say: "Wordless cognitive awareness is a remarkable instrument that helps us open the gates of wisdom". It is the key to the levels of transcendental and abstract samādhi of the Prajñā Pāramitā school of Buddhism. Only when we have developed our wordless cognitive awareness will we have sufficient capability to apply in samādhi abstract and transcendental topics such as Suchness, Emptiness, Formlessness, and Wishlessness, etc.

Conclusion

In summary, together with the practice of Zen, we need to also practice Qi Gong to support our Zen practice. We will only be able to sample the taste of the Zen cake when we have experienced samādhi (stillness of mind) in a stable manner, clearly recognized the true characteristics of worldly phenomena, totally transformed our perspective on life, and started to gradually develop our spiritual wisdom.

COMMENTARY TREATISE 5:

A NEW CONCEPT OF ZEN PRACTICE

A New Concept of Zen Practice

This is an important explanatory article. It defines the Zen method that I prescribe while also pointing out the differences between my method and other methods. Nowadays, Zen has become a movement widespread in many developed countries such as the USA, Germany, France, Switzerland, etc., as well as countries with deep-rooted traditions in Buddhism such as Sri Lanka, Myanmar, Thailand, Mongolia, Japan, Taiwan, Korea, and Vietnam. As there are many schools of Buddhist spiritual cultivation and practice, I need to define the practice method that I teach so that students can clearly understand it.

Key focus of new concept

I call my method "new concept" as it goes against the old concept espoused by many Zen traditions of the past centuries or decades. In reality, it is old for it is the method that the Buddha established. We are following the Buddha's teaching to practice and apply it in our everyday life. What is new is the combination of the Buddha's teaching with modern science in our practice, as well as not following the model of some Zen traditions that over-stimulate the sympathetic nervous system while neglecting the parasympathetic nervous system.

Specifically, the new concept is built upon six points:

1. Role of definitions

Before I study or teach a topic, I always clearly define the topic. If the topic is not well defined, we will make mistakes when we practice it. In our physical travel, we can easily correct an error of navigation, but if we lose our way on the Zen path we may develop mental troubles. These are disorders within the nervous system which result in psychosomatic illnesses such as diabetes, high blood pressure, irregular heartbeat, or stroke and may eventually lead to death as the illnesses do their damage.

With any topic, I always start with definitions, and then go deeper into explanations and practice instructions. Definitions are very important to the Zen practitioner in the same way as a compass is to the ship captain.

Definitions about a topic can usually be of three types:

1. Academic definitions

2. Circular definitions

3. Popular definitions

- Academic definitions are lofty and philosophical. They help the listener gain broader knowledge and sophisticated literature references but are removed from practicality. When we try to use them to guide our practice, we will find that it is like trying to *climb mountains by grabbing at moss.*

Example:

Question: What is samādhi?

Answer: Samādhi is the unified mind, in which there is only a single-thought awareness. Samādhi is the one-pointed mind. The one-pointed mind is the mind that dwells on a single matter. A mind that dwells on a single matter is a mind that focuses its attention on an object.

- A circular definition is one that keeps talking about the topic without exhausting ideas and without reaching an end. The listener will also find it difficult to put the topic into practice.

Example:

Question: What is samādhi?

Answer: Samādhi is the mind devoid of false thoughts. A mind devoid of false thoughts is a mind that is not stuck in dualism. A mind not stuck in dualism is a mind that is not disorderly or scattered. The eight winds cannot trouble it, etc.

- A popular definition is one that is easy to understand, easy to know, and easy to recognize. It is also easy to apply, as it accords with the level of knowledge of the vast majority of people.

Example:

Question: What is samādhi?

Answer: It is wordless awareness

Question: How can I practice it?

Answer: You practice it by stopping the verbal chatter in the mind.

2. Role of harmony

Zen focuses on a practice that leads to a transformation of the mind, alleviation of illnesses of the body, and development of spiritual wisdom. This will eventually lead to harmony between the practitioner's body and mind, then harmony with people surrounding them, and harmony with the surrounding environment which consists of human society and the natural environment. If you practice Zen but have not manifested this experiential harmony through your attitude, gestures, and speech toward other people and events, you need to revisit your method of practicing Zen.

This is why I elevate harmony as the most important point in Zen. It is both the result of a practice based on wordless awareness and the catalyst for spiritual development of the individual and security and order of the society in which we live.

Under the new concept of Zen practice, I teach students many ways to experience harmony in their own body and mind. These methods impact on the parasympathetic nervous system through processes associated with *awareness* and *cognitive awareness*.

A person who has not experienced harmony within their own body and mind cannot have harmony with other people. This is because the selfish nature is still latent in the mind of the un-awakened person. They like to see faults in others while never having the courage to see their own faults and correct them.

Sorrow, suffering, dispute, struggle, argument, perversion, delusion, and attachment all originate from disharmony within our body and mind, itself caused by our inability to develop the energy of awareness from our Wordless Awareness Mind.

3. *Role of relaxation*

Zen does not prescribe oppressing the body or oppressing the mind but instead *relaxing body and mind* by developing the energy of awareness, Silent Awareness, Awake Awareness and Cognitive Awareness.

This is why I always prescribe the following when I teach the practice of any topic:

- Do not exert too much effort, do not emulate the ancients who "pasted the word death on their forehead" to remind themselves that they must exert maximal effort, no matter day or night, and were determined to succeed even if they had to die.

- Do not attach importance to concentrating the mind or focusing attention on the topic.

- Do not use imagination to contemplate worldly phenomena.

- Do not use auto-suggestion as a means to *crush the grass with a rock* or to *watch the mouse like a cat*.

By contrast, I prescribe:

- Practice *leisurely but regularly*, by applying *awareness* in everyday activities.

- Use self-discipline: have a half-hour sitting meditation session early in the morning and another in the evening before going to bed.

- Besides these set sessions, practice in the four postures: when driving, passing water, sitting idly, getting dressed, washing the car, having a shower, eating, or washing the dishes, etc. At any moment we can use our awareness.

This is our practice method to reach directly the Wordless Awareness Mind through various awareness processes: single-thought awareness, wordless awareness, silent awareness, awake awareness, and cognitive awareness (which is an attribute of Buddha-nature).

We do not meander around in our practice because we will be wasting our time and then end up with an ill body, disturbed mind, and non-creative intellect instead of our desired destination of a healthy body, peaceful mind, and bright insights and wisdom.

We need to remember this point when we apply our new concept of Zen. Only when we are able to maintain the wordless awareness processes will we be able to experience deep and stable samādhi states. Through these samādhi states, we will be able to experience elation and bliss, tranquility of body and mind, transformation of the mind, and harmony in body and mind.

The principle of spiritual wisdom development is founded upon wordless awareness processes.

In summary, in Zen, relaxation is the antidote for almost all illnesses of the body and mind and is the means by which spiritual wisdom lights up. Creativity is founded on this principle.

When we truly experience a relaxed mind, the afflictions of attachment and clinging to falsehood are blown away. We will experience serenity, joy, and harmony in our mind. In Zen, a serene mind is a crucial factor helping us develop our spiritual wisdom.

The opposite of a serene mind is a mind with attachment, subjectivity, and full of prejudices, fixed opinions, and biases toward other people and events.

How can we experience a relaxed mind? We can use the relaxing-the-tongue exercise, or practice the wordless awareness processes in the four postures or the breathing steps under the Awareness-of-breathing-in-and-breathing-out Samādhi method (ānapānasati samādhi).

Question: Master, could you please explain the relaxing-the-mind method through the wordless awareness processes?

Answer: Each time our senses come into contact with an external object, we make sure that we only have an awareness of it in an objective manner. This is the first flash of awareness, which is wordless. We do not follow it with any thinking, differentiating comparison, inferring, or speculating on the object. In this way, our awareness stops at the Feelings and Sensations aggregate. This is the way to relax the mind or relax the thinking in our first Zen practice step. We can apply this method in the four postures.

Question: Master, ordinarily every time we see an object we immediately name it, so how can we relax the mind or relax the thinking?

Answer: It is true that this is the naming habit that we have gained and repeated since we were a baby, when our parents started to teach us to name things. In school through to adulthood we have continuously developed this internal talk habit by thinking, arguing, differentiating, comparing, and judging. As a result, internal talk has become a very strong habit that I call "the language pathway in the mind".

If we now want to see an object without silently naming it, we need to practice for a long time to form a new habit in our mind, the habit of *no talk*. We will then be able to experience immediately what is relaxing the mind or relaxing the thinking.

4. Role of science and the brain

We borrow scientific knowledge to reconcile our practice with the Buddha's teaching. In this way, we will be able to demonstrate the validity of the Buddha's teaching to people of all levels of spiritual development. We know why we are practicing incorrectly and why we are practicing correctly. We know the result of an incorrect or a correct practice. We do not blame past karma when we incur illnesses of the body and mind or see no illumination of spiritual wisdom in our Zen practice.

For example, we rely on the knowledge of what biochemical substances are released in the endocrine system, the sympathetic and parasympathetic nervous systems, and brainstem, to ascertain whether we are practicing correctly or incorrectly a practical exercise or meditation technique. Illnesses will decrease if we did it correctly and will increase if we did it incorrectly.

In addition, we can use an electroencephalogram (EEG) machine to know whether a practical exercise or meditation technique actually results in a beta, alpha, theta or delta brainwave in order to ascertain its validity.

The teaching of the Buddha is always correct. Our inability to experience harmony within our body and mind, harmony with the surrounding environment, and development of the energy of wisdom from our Wordless Awareness Mind and Buddha-nature is merely caused by us applying an incorrect technique that impacts on the wrong nervous system or brain structure area.

How do we know that our practice is correct? We know that it is correct if we do not use our sensory organs to concentrate on the object, instead using the practical exercises of Knowing, or Just Knowing, etc. These exercises cause the activation of the parasympathetic nervous system, resulting in the release of acetylcholine.

Nowadays, when we practice Zen, we need to rely on our knowledge of the brain to know exactly how the brain areas associated with the False Mind and True Mind get activated; from where inner talk (vitakka) and inner dialogue (vicāra) arise; the characteristics of the False Mind; the characteristics of the True Mind; how we dwell in the True Mind; how we vanquish the False Mind; how passions and addictions accumulate in our brain.

By looking at the brain, we will recognize the cascading interaction between the mind, teaching, techniques, cerebral cortex, limbic system, endocrine system, and biochemical substances.

These parts belong in contemporary knowledge, that we need to add to our tools in order to avoid mistakes when we practice.

This important point leads me to describe in general the human anatomy consisting of the brain, nervous system, endocrine system, and internal organs and how they react to the psychological and emotional impact of our mental states (*cetasika*).

Once we gain this basic knowledge, we will easily understand the biofeedback principle in Zen. The value of

Zen resides in this point. If we do not understand the action and effect principle between the mind, teaching, brain, and techniques, we will easily make mistakes when we practice or use auto-suggestion methods.

5. Direct approach

My direct approach means that we do not go around in circles but aim straight at the Wordless Awareness Mind structure. In a short period of time, we will be able to have some experience of peacefulness and alleviation of psychosomatic illnesses.

I have designed several practical exercises that I jokingly call "fire extinguishers" or "instant noodles". Examples are: Looking at Sunlight, Looking at Darkness, Hearing Sounds, Two-pace Breathing, etc. These are ways to aim straight at our target.

Tools

In order to *aim straight* when we practice, we need to equip ourselves with a thorough understanding of the Three Aspects of Knowing topic, and then the concepts of sensory response and biofeedback in Zen.

In regard to the biochemical substances that are secreted in our body, we need to know:

1. Which gland secretes which substance?

2. What effect does this substance have on our internal organs and well-being?

3. How do we stop, regulate, or increase the release of this substance through our Zen practice?

There are four substances that usually cause the chronic illnesses that modern medicine has difficulty overcoming, such as high blood pressure, obesity, chronic insomnia, diabetes, depression, memory loss, and Parkinson's disease. These four substances are norepinephrine (or noradrenaline), epinephrine (or adrenaline), glucagon, and cortisol.

However, there are also substances secreted in the brain, at nerve endings of the parasympathetic nervous system and in endocrine glands that can help the body recover its balance and alleviate the above-mentioned illnesses. These include serotonin, acetylcholine, melatonin, dopamine, and insulin.

Question: Master, could you please explain what you mean by "go straight"?

Answer: When I say "go straight", I mean that we aim directly at our desired destination when we practice. Let us take as an example the situation where we have chronic insomnia. We know that this situation is caused by a dysfunction of the group of nuclei in the hypothalamus that regulate the sleep-wake cycle. This dysfunction causes the nuclei to stop releasing melatonin, and this is the reason for our insomnia.

We have two practical exercises to address this situation: (1) Looking at sunlight and (2) Looking at darkness. With the first exercise, by looking at sunlight reflected on a surface such as the courtyard for about 15 minutes, we will cause the pineal gland to release serotonin and melatonin. With the second exercise, by looking at darkness for 15 to 30 minutes, we will cause the hypothalamus to release melatonin which in turn causes us to feel sleepy and then fall asleep.

Question: And Master, what do you mean by aiming straight at the Wordless Awareness Mind?

Answer: We know that the function of the Wordless Awareness Mind is wordless awareness through the three ultimate faculties: Ultimate Seeing, Ultimate Hearing and Ultimate Touch. For example, when we practice the Hearing the Bell exercise, we will just maintain the awareness of hearing, without any comment or thinking. We will then activate the wordless awareness of Ultimate Hearing.

As another example, when we practice the Two-pace Breathing exercise, we are just silently aware of breathing in, silently aware of breathing out, and do not do any counting in our mind, nor do we follow the breath with our mind. This wordless awareness signal will activate the Ultimate Touch faculty of the Wordless Awareness Mind.

Question: Master, could you please give an example of an exercise that aims straight at Ultimate Seeing?

Answer: When we look at an object and know the object clearly but without silently naming it in our mind, we will generate a signal that goes straight to Ultimate Seeing.

6. *Role of practical exercises and meditation techniques*

Whether our Zen practice will have good or poor results, go fast or slow, go straight or around in a circle depends on practical exercises and meditation techniques.

The teaching may be sublime, but if we do not master the practical exercises and meditation techniques, we will never be able to experience the taste of the Zen cake.

Among the four Zen practice methods, only anupassanā (contemplation) does not involve practical exercises and meditation techniques. The other three methods, samatha (tranquility), samādhi (stillness of mind) and paññā (wisdom) all make use of practical exercises and meditation techniques.

This is why we need to be thoroughly proficient with practical exercises and meditation techniques.

Question: Master, could you please explain the difference between practical exercises and meditation techniques?

Answer: Practical exercises are short and concise exercises that do not require a lot of time and have immediate results; these I have called "fire extinguishers" or "instant noodles". For example, if you suffer from chronic insomnia, you can practice Looking at Darkness and immediately alleviate this problem. Or if you suffer from high blood pressure, you can practice Two-Pace Breathing or Hearing the Bell and see your blood pressure gradually balance itself. Or if you suffer from depression, you can practice Looking at Sunlight and see your depression go away. These are examples of how to apply practical exercises.

On the other hand, with meditation techniques, you need to practice assiduously over a long period of time to see good results. For example, if you want to have the Wordless Awareness Mind permanently present in your daily life, you will need to understand first what the Wordless Awareness Mind is, where it operates in our brain, and what its characteristics and functions are. You will then need to apply a meditation technique that accords with the Wordless Awareness Mind. For example, a characteristic of the Wordless Awareness Mind is wordless self-awareness. Once you have identified this characteristic, you can apply a technique that develops awareness without any chatter in the mind. Once you have attained this state of mind, you have accomplished wordless awareness.

Question: Master, could you please summarize the key point of the new concept of Zen practice?

Answer: The most important point is that I have shone the light of Western neuroscience onto the Eastern Zen method to highlight its marvelous values.

Question: Master, could you please tell us what these marvelous values are?

Answer: First, when we practice Zen we know exactly what functions of the brain are activated, what biochemical substances are secreted, and how these substances contribute to our well-being. For example, the Buddha taught us to just maintain awareness when we breathe. We now know that by doing so, a signal will activate Ultimate Touch while simultaneously activating the parasympathetic nervous system; acetylcholine will be released at the nerve endings of the parasympathetic nervous system, which will impact on internal organs and the endocrine system, etc.

Second, we know the reason why spiritual wisdom develops. With the breathing method for example, if we practice regularly, we will experience a clear cognitive awareness while our mind is immobile. This is the state of Immobility Samādhi, or the Tathā-Mind, which is a function of the precuneus located in the parietal lobe of the cerebral cortex, on both the left and right hemispheres. From there, our potential for enlightenment will gradually develop.

Question: Master, could you please tell us how you define Zen under the new concept?

Answer: I define Zen as the art of *training brain cells* into the new habit of silence.

Question: Master, what practice topic do we use to train our brain cells into the habit of silence?

Answer: In Zen, there are many practice topics or practice methods to achieve this result. I propose a unified topic to guide students straight into the wordless awareness character of the Wordless Awareness Mind. It is the "No Talk" topic.

"No Talk" is an order telling brain cells not to have any inner talk. When it is assiduously repeated many times over a long period of time, it becomes a code that is stored in our long term memory as well as our wordless cognitive awareness area, which is the precuneus. Once the code "No Talk" is immanent in our precuneus, all we need to do is use our cognition to evoke the "no talk state" and all our brain cells will become immobile.

Question: Master, what do you mean by immanent?

Answer: Immanent means being present in something, or being stored in something through a long process of practice that has happened beforehand.

Question: Master, why do all our brain cells become immediately immobile when we evoke the "No Talk" state?

Answer: It is because our brain cells have the characteristic of being interconnected. When we evoke "No Talk", this signal immediately enters the brain through the three relay stations and instantaneously propagates to all parts of the

A NEW CONCEPT OF ZEN PRACTICE 141

brain. This is due to the interconnectedness of brain cells. This interconnectedness is also the reason why I say that Zen is the art of training brain cells into the new habit of silence.

Question: Master, does this state where all brain cells are immobile correspond to Immobility Samādhi?

Answer: This state is indeed the fourth stage of samādhi attained by the Buddha, which is called Immobility Samādhi, or the Right Samādhi (in the Noble Eightfold Path), or Signless Samādhi (part of the Three Gates to Liberation taught by the Buddha), or Diamond Samādhi, or Suchness Samādhi, or Non-abiding Samādhi (according to Developmental Buddhism).

COMMENTARY TREATISE 6:

FOUR RELAY STATIONS IN THE

HUMAN BRAIN

First Relay Station: Reticular Formation

Functions

Research on anatomy and the brain by scientists specialized in this field attributes the following functions to the "reticular formation":

1. Relay station. It relays sensory information sent from receptors in the tongue, eyes, ears and body (skin, bones, and muscles) to the thalamus and conveys directional information that it receives from sensory organs to the cerebellum for it to establish body balance and the source of the information. Due to this relay function, it is considered to be part of the recognition system, meaning that it recognizes the object or external or internal environment without going through the cerebral cortex. For example, when the ears hear a sound, the reticular formation recognizes the type of sound and the direction of its source while the pre-frontal cortex (which includes the thinking and differentiating consciousness areas) has not had the time to intervene. Likewise, when the eyes see a fire, it immediately recognizes the nature of this fire and alerts the cerebral cortex through the thalamus of its importance or ordinariness.

2. Alerting mechanism. Based on the previous function of the reticular formation, neuroscientists have attributed to it the second function of "alerting". However this alerting is not necessarily accurate. For example, if the eyes see a rope and send it the incorrect information about something that looks like a snake, it will still alert to the presence of a snake. Although this alerting is not accurate, it still raises the vigilance of the cerebral cortex toward these events or other information that the reticular formation receives from

FOUR RELAY STATIONS IN THE HUMAN BRAIN 145

the four sensory organs. For this reason, severe damage to the reticular formation leads to a state of coma, whereas light damage leads to a loss of consciousness about the environment. In contrast, when we are deep in sleep and the reticular formation suddenly receives a strong signal, we will wake up immediately and develop an appropriate response to the information that we received while in deep sleep.

3. Maintain wakefulness and alertness. Psychologists and neuroscientists have defined this state as the state of being aroused and alert about something that is about to happen and which may have an adverse effect on the self. This is a higher function of the reticular formation. It reflects the state of arousal of the individual. It helps us have a state of conscious arousal that allows us to have an appropriate response when we come into contact with the surrounding environment without involving the pre-frontal cortex areas. It fulfills this role through its interconnection with the hypothalamus which has the ability to express states of the False Mind as well as of the True Mind. Although the reticular formation does not have the ability to activate muscles, it still contributes to the expression of attitudes such as trembling, lethargy, alertness, swiftness or leisureliness, indifference or tenseness. It brings the cerebral cortex into accord with the external environment and the state of internal anxiety. This is its wakefulness function. In its role as a relay station, the reticular formation acts as a filter for sensory information that comes from the external environment or internal organs and then transmits it to the thalamus or down to the internal organs. If it fails to transmit information, biological reactions of the body will not manifest (such as having bone chills or goose bumps when we are under the illusion that there are ghosts

146 FOUR RELAY STATIONS IN THE HUMAN BRAIN

around when we hear rustling sounds at night outside the meditation hall).

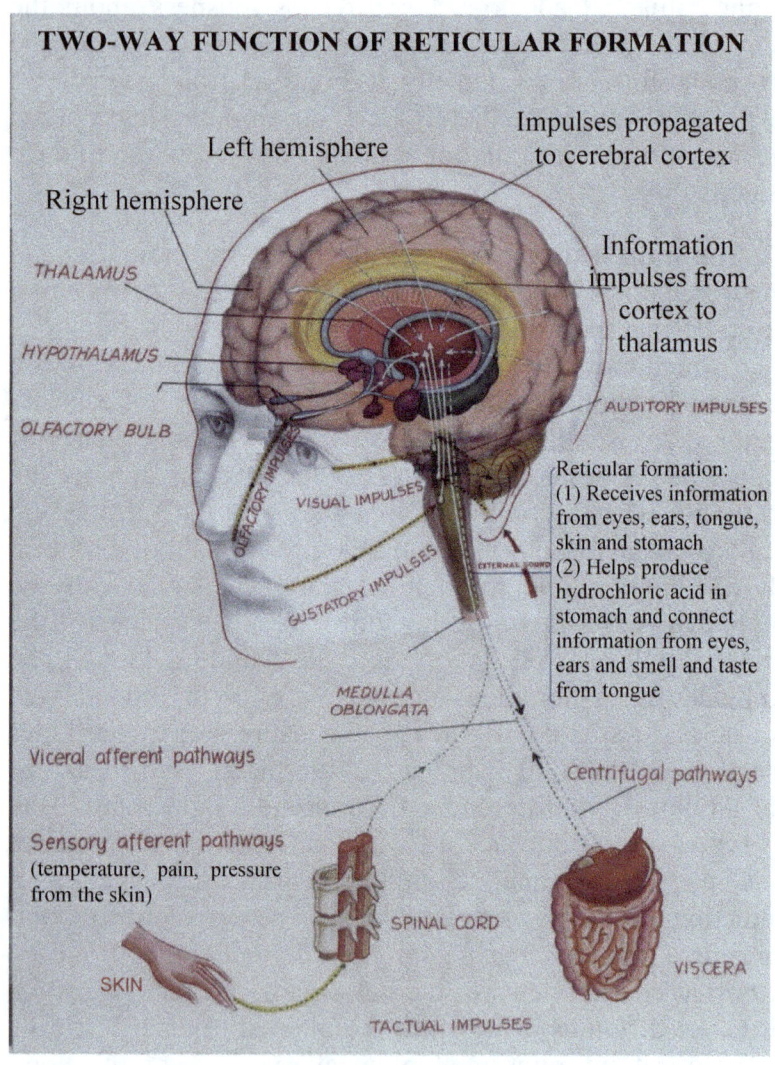

4. Overall management of the wakefulness of the cortex. A conscious arousal, as defined by neuroscience and psychology, is the state of being awake and aware while being able to make judgments and distinctions. This is the special function of a group of nerve cells in the reticular formation that have two-way interactions with the hypothalamus, cerebellum and spinal cord. For this reason, this group of nerve cells is attributed the role of overall management of the wakefulness of the cerebral cortex. For example, a network of nerve cells may send a series of signals to the cortex through the hypothalamus, but if the reticular formation does not transmit these signals, the cortex will not receive them. Neuroscientists and psychologists call this group of nerve cells the "reticular activating system". All signals from sensory organs transit through the reticular activating system before continuing to the thalamus and then the cerebral cortex; however it may choose to ignore the signals and not pass them on. (This explains why many students can study in the university cafeteria as they are not affected or irritated by the constant noise generated by people coming and going and using their cutlery at their table while their sensory organs still capture all the sights and sounds. Similarly, we can often see Indian yogi sitting in meditation at busy intersections where a lot of people and vehicles pass by. More clearly still, when you are engrossed in an espionage or martial arts novel, you will know nothing about what is happening around you.) The reticular activating system can also initiate an alert about something unusual that may happen, so that the cerebral cortex pays attention or increases vigilance. As an example, you are walking along the footpath and have no knowledge that the wristband of your watch has come loose. However if the tightening on your wrist suddenly lessens, the sensory signal from your wrist will reach the reticular activating system which draws your attention to the fact that your watch is about to drop! If the reticular activating system does not act as a filter but transmits all sensory signals to the cerebral cortex, you will immediately become confused. This situation arises when the reticular activating system has been weakened and becomes unable to filter the information. This explains why sometimes in their sleep, monks and nuns think that they are still lay people and dream of things that are forbidden in their code of conduct, such as partaking in feasts with a lot of animal products or enjoying the pleasures of the flesh.

Furthermore, the reticular activating system will not be able to fulfill its role if it is impacted by the sleep-inducing center in the hypothalamus which results in you feeling sleepy. If you are in this situation and continue your sitting meditation, you may fall asleep. Only when you have learnt to maintain your awareness through practicing samatha (tranquility) or samādhi (stillness of mind) will your sleep-inducing center cease to impact on your reticular activating system.

The reticular activating system is also weakened by alcohol, sleep tablets, anesthetic medications, and cigarette addiction.

This shows that the management function of the reticular activating system depends also on subjective factors such as avoiding alcohol and tobacco, and practicing taking control of your thinking. Scientists do not discuss these factors and only identify the functions of the reticular activating system.

5. Focusing the attention. Under the influence of the cerebral cortex, not only does the reticular formation control our wakefulness, vigilance and awareness, it also helps us achieve an efficient focusing of attention through its direct relation to the four sensory organs: eyes, ears, tongue, and body. When you practice one of the Yoga or Buddhist (Theravāda, Developmental or Zen Buddhism) breath control techniques, you are actually using the attention energy of the reticular formation because it directs the whole breathing-in and breathing-out mechanism, while the cerebral cortex (the Thinking Faculty area) plays the role of conductor. For this reason, one needs to use the correct method when practicing focusing on the breath in order to achieve a high level of effectiveness.

Yoga and the various schools of Buddhism often use the eyes and ears to focus the attention on a topic, and in doing so, they use or go through the reticular formation. When Qi Gong practitioners concentrate their attention to "move the vital energy", unblock meridians, or cure inner trauma, they are using the reticular formation. When athletes train their muscles and body movements in running, swimming, boxing, etc., they too use the reticular formation's attention-focusing function.

6. Control. The reticular formation is capable of controlling bodily functions such as respiration and blood circulation, as well as monitoring and adjusting the sensory information that comes from the external environment. For example, it controls the normal breathing of a person, i.e. the breathing that occurs when the person does not focus their attention onto controlling the breath. When the alveoli (air sacs) in the lungs lack oxygen, the reticular formation will direct related systems such as the diaphragm and rib cage muscles to take a deep breath without needing any directive from the cerebral cortex. For this reason, when a meditator achieves a no-thought state, they experience the phenomenon of "quiet breathing" or "pure breathing" in which their lungs suddenly take a deep breath. When the alveoli lack oxygen (according to a certain density threshold), they activate the breathing-in activating center in the medulla oblongata which initiates a reflex action by relevant systems to take in a deep breath.

In ancient times (and even nowadays), yogi and fakir in India are capable of controlling the reticular formation by using their will to direct the breathing centers in the brain stem and medulla oblongata. For this reason, they managed to survive on the small amount of oxygen contained in their coffin when they were buried underground for several days. However, they would certainly die of lack of oxygen if they went beyond the pre-determined length of time.

Conclusion

The reticular formation is a special nervous structure that plays the role of intermediary between the mind and mental states (cetasika). Without it, we cannot lead a normal life. From time immemorial, Easterners have known how to exploit its special functions to regulate body and mind through breathing techniques and to alert sensory organs through the contemplation method, even though they did not recognize its specific functions like modern Western scientists do.

Zen practitioners of the modern era need to combine the Eastern and Western experiences to generate supporting causal conditions that help their practice become more efficient and avoid wasting time finding their way as in ancient times.

Although the reticular formation is just a nerve network approximately 12 cm long (just a little longer than the index finger of an adult person) located in the brain stem, it plays an important role in controlling our attention and arousal.

When we practice walking meditation and focus on every step and every movement with arousal and wakefulness, we are using the capability of the reticular formation. Likewise when we concentrate on the contemplation of a topic, such as contemplating the Three Characteristics of Worldly Phenomena, at that very moment we are using the function of the reticular formation. This means that we are not using the effort of the Consciousness. When a person reaches the state of awareness or clear awareness, they are really in control of the reticular formation. External conditions (i.e. the four objects of the four senses of seeing, hearing, taste and touch) cannot affect them. While they may be meditating in a noisy and busy place, sounds are not transmitted to their thalamus.

References

in relation to the reticular formation

1. Bevan, James 1978, *Anatomy and Physiology*, USA, pp. 59-60, 62, 92.

2. Diamond, M.C., Scheibel A. B. and Elson, L. M. 1984, *The Human Brain*, USA, pp. 4-19.

3. Eccles, John C. 1992, *The Human Psyche*, USA, pp. 142-145, 163.

4. Hirai, Tomio 1989, *Zen Meditation and Psychology*, USA, p. 121.

5. Juhan, Deane 1987, *Job's Body*, USA, p. 216.

6. Kagan and Havemann 1976, *Psychology, an Introduction*, USA, pp. 253-254.

7. Marieb, Elaine N. 1992, *Human Anatomy and Physiology*, USA, pp. 402, 487.

8. Muun, Norman L. 1956, *Psychology*, USA, pp. 63, 263, 362, 565.

9. Myers, David G. 1990, *Exploring Psychology*, USA, pp. 29-30.

10. Posner, Michael I. and Raichle, Marcus E. 1994, *Images of Mind*, USA, p. 210.

11. Restak, Richard M. 1984, *The Brain*, USA, pp. 129, 314, 317.

12. Rossi, Ernest L. and Cheek, David B. 1988, *Mind-Body Therapy*, USA, p. 21.

13. Ruch, Patton, Woodbury and Towe 1984, *Neurophysiology*, USA, pp. 216, 218.

14. Sinelnikov, R. D. 1990, *Atlas of Human Anatomy, Vol. III*, Moscow, pp. 26, 48, 75.

15. Truex, Raymond C. and Carpenter, Malcolm B. 1969, *Human Neuroanatomy*, USA, pp. 6, 280, 298, 319, 324, 338, 362, 364, 394-401, 465-466.

16. Weber, Ann L. 1990, *Psychology, an Introduction*, USA, p. 53.

Second Relay Station: Thalamus

OVERVIEW

Composition

The thalamus is part of the limbic system.

Location

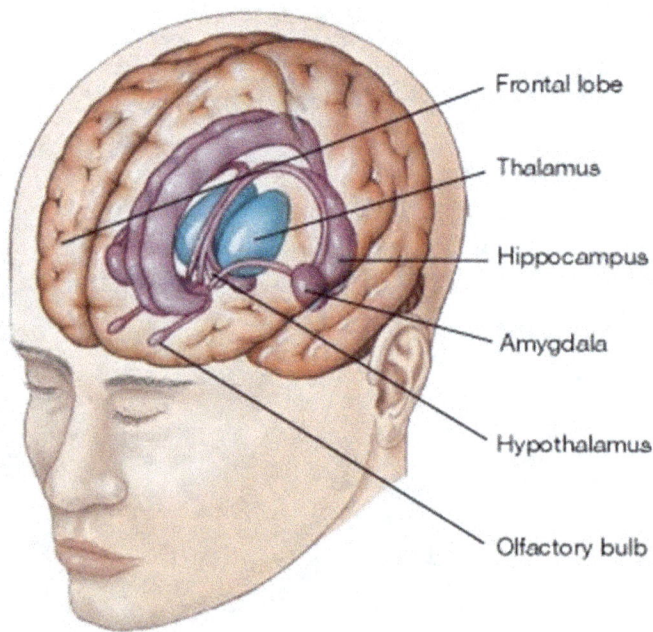

The thalamus, together with the hypothalamus, constitutes the diencephalon or the "between brain", because of its location between the two hemispheres of the brain and the midbrain. Thalamus in Greek means the "chamber" or "resting place"; the two hemispheres of the brain safely *rest* on it. Due to its central position in the brain and its role as the place through which all sensory signals must pass on their way to the cerebral cortex (except for smell signals which go first to the hypothalamus before getting to the thalamus), it is the most notable of relay stations and contains many groups of nuclei with specific functions. Scientists have named these groups of nuclei according to their function in the transmission of signals to relevant locations. These groups of nuclei provide basic interpretation or basic awareness of sensory signals that they receive and disseminate to relevant destinations.

The following structures transmit information to the thalamus:

- The reticular formation, which transmits sensory signals of sight, sound, taste, and touch.

- The hypothalamus, which transmits sensory signals of smell, as well as emotions and sensations from internal organs.

- The cerebellum, which transmits information for maintaining body balance.

- The somatosensory motor cortex, which transmits motor signals to internal organs, limbs, and body.

Functions

The main function of the thalamus is to:

- Receive and transmit sensory signals to the frontal lobes, parietal lobes, occipital lobes, and temporal lobes.

- Act as intermediary for sensory, motor, cortex wakefulness, and memory functions.

Remark: The thalamus is the gate to the cerebral cortex. The "outline of the six objects of senses" goes through it; bodily karma and speech karma are also transmitted through its *gate*. I consider it to be the second relay station. It plays an important role in disseminating sensory information to other parts of the brain, regulating awareness, alertness, attention and emotional content of sensory experience. (The reticular formation is the first relay station). If we consider the consciousness model of the Consciousness School of Buddhism, the term Transferred Consciousness would correspond to the function of the thalamus.

Third Relay Station: Hypothalamus

The hypothalamus is a fascinating structure in a small area of the limbic system, situated inside the brain, behind the eyes, below (hypo) the thalamus and above the pituitary gland. Its position below the thalamus earns it its name of hypothalamus. The hypothalamus is an essential part of the diencephalon together with the thalamus. It is the center that regulates the function of internal organs.

Weight

Despite weighing just four grams, representing $1/300^{th}$ of the mass of the brain and $1/100^{th}$ of the volume of the external brain, the hypothalamus plays a role in all areas of human behavior such as hunger, thirst, sexual functions, sleep, body temperature, emotional states, endocrine functions, and movement.

Functions

Despite its small size and weight of just four grams, the hypothalamus plays a very important role in our life. It regulates all functions of our body and mind due to its role in regulating our consciousness, emotional states, and internal organ functions. It helps keep our body healthy and our skin rosy, but can also generate psychosomatic illnesses and cause the body to look decrepit and emaciated. This is due to its direct connections to the endocrine system and autonomic nervous system. The hypothalamus is considered a higher autonomic center and the master gland of the endocrine system.

As the axon of nerve cells of nuclei groups in the hypothalamus extends to sympathetic and parasympathetic centers in the brain stem, impulses generated in the hypothalamus can stimulate or inhibit the lower autonomic centers. In other words, the hypothalamus coordinates, regulates, and controls autonomic activities in the body. It is the link between the mind, brain, and body, as well as the link between the nervous system and the endocrine system. It also contains centers related to appetite, thirst, and sex.

The hypothalamus functions as a main relay station between the cerebral cortex and lower autonomic centers. Impulses from centers in the cerebral cortex reach the hypothalamus. Then through many synapse pathways in the hypothalamus, these impulses are relayed onto pathways leading to autonomic centers in the brain stem and lower centers in the spinal cord. Through its role as the link between the cerebral cortex and lower centers, the hypothalamus acts as the link between the mind and body. Emotions channeled through it change body functions. It is an important relay station along nerve pathways that convey the mind's influence to the whole body, which may sometimes, unfortunately, generate psychosomatic illnesses.

Role of centers

As a brief summary, the hypothalamus consists of nine centers, each consisting of groups of nuclei. Scientists have identified approximately 22 small groups of nuclei that form the following main centers.

1. Response to emotions and expression as body, speech and thought behaviors

The hypothalamus acts as a compere to express all emotions such as sadness, joy, anger, screaming, crying, praying, insulting, abusing, trembling, shivering, turning red with anger, turning pale with fear, heart stopping, fainting, rudeness, violence, lust, gluttony, fight or flight, stealing, looting, aggression, invasion, repentance or regret, gentle or quiet, effective or slow, etc. In contrast, if we attain samādhi (stillness of mind), our True Mind emerges and our mind becomes calm, equanimous, spontaneous, and tranquil, the hypothalamus will also express these states of mind through our body and speech.

2. It is the monitoring and control center for all activities of the body and mind, through its control of the autonomic nervous system that impacts on blood pressure, heart rate, deep or shallow breathing, and gut and internal organ motility.

The hypothalamus is seen as a multi-purpose structure of the central nervous system. Without it, the central nervous system or our mind (the False Mind in Zen) cannot express the true substance of emotions and sensations. For example, if you are screaming at someone but do not express any anger content, this screaming does not affect your internal organs. It is as if you are pretending to be angry; you may be screaming but do not feel any anger inside. However, if you are really angry, the anger impulse will reach the hypothalamus which will immediately express all aspects related to anger to your internal organs as well as gestures in your arms, legs, head, face, look, lips, mouth, and tone of voice.

In principle, the hypothalamus operates under the control of the central nervous system consisting of the Thinking Faculty (located in the left pre-frontal cortex) and the differentiating Consciousness (located in the right pre-frontal cortex). If these two areas do not send impulses that have a wholesome/unwholesome or right/wrong content to it, it will remain silent. In reality, however, the hypothalamus also receives information from other areas of the brain such as olfactory receptors in the nose that send signals to it first, and working memory areas, emotional memory areas (the amygdala) and long term memory areas in the limbic system which also send information to it first without going through the Thinking Faculty. All these signals result in physiological states in the body.

For this reason, the hypothalamus is dubbed "the neural clearinghouse" by neuroscientists, to illustrate its role in receiving information from the five sensory organs, the external environment (such as the weather), internal organs, and the central nervous system, and then sending signals to the autonomic nervous system and the endocrine system to initiate a response to the information that it sent.

The hypothalamus links with the anterior pituitary through the portal venous system to excite the pituitary into releasing six hormones. It also controls the posterior pituitary through a nerve.

In addition, it has a monitoring and regulating role over the autonomic nervous system that consists of the sympathetic and parasympathetic nervous systems. For example, when we suddenly receive an alert or a stimulus, the central nervous system sends a signal to the hypothalamus which activates the sympathetic nervous system into sending impulses to internal organs that cause the heart rate to increase, the breath to quicken, irises to enlarge, and blood to flow into muscles to increase their size. The medical term for this state is the *fight or flight response*.

3. In addition, it has several groups of nerve cells associated with the control or regulation of body temperature, such as feeling hot or cold (resulting in sweating or shivering). For this reason it is considered the temperature regulating center of the body. Its anterior region deals with sweating and its posterior region with shivering.

4. It also regulates the water level in the body.

5. It regulates the feeling of satiety.

6. It regulates the sleep-wake cycle. The suprachiasmatic nuclei (SCN) control the circadian rhythms of the body, (including the release of melatonin), sleep-wake cycles, and body temperature rhythm.

7. Its other and most important function is to **coordinate the function of the endocrine system** through the pituitary gland, resulting in a healthy body.

Due to these important and practical characteristics of the hypothalamus, modern psychologists and psychoanalysts have promoted the practice of Yoga and Buddhist meditation techniques using the methods of anupassanā (contemplation), samatha (tranquility), samādhi (stillness of mind) and paññā (wisdom) to treat psychosomatic illnesses by acting on the hypothalamus.

Conclusion

Within the brain, the hypothalamus is a mass of grey matter that represents only $1/300^{th}$ of the volume of the brain but is seen as the center for expressing mental and emotional states as well as biological states of the body under stimulation from the cerebral cortex:

- The pre-frontal areas on both left and right hemispheres.

- The areas of the three ultimate faculties of the Wordless Awareness Mind.

- The Ultimate Cognitive Awareness area in the parietal lobe and precuneus.

- The limbic system, thalamus, olfactory organs, and brain stem consisting of the reticular formation and impulses from internal organs through the spinal cord.

In mental processes where false thoughts do not arise, the hypothalamus generates blood activation states and impacts on the endocrine system to help us alleviate psychological or psychosomatic illnesses such as diabetes, high blood pressure, nervous breakdown, stomach ulcers, etc. The result is a healthy body and peaceful mind. Zen's concept of transformation of the mind starts with the hypothalamus, *provided that the Wordless Awareness Mind is present*, for it generates biological actions that help us eliminate mental defilements/old habits and alleviate psychosomatic illnesses. In this context, it represents the White Buffalo symbolizing the True Mind in Chinese Zen literature.

From the karma perspective, the hypothalamus is part of the Mental Formation aggregate as it expresses all the states of the False Mind through bodily action (which involves the arm, leg, body, head, face, eye, skin, and internal organs) and speech action (which includes the tonality of crying, screaming, soothing, wailing, insult, or irritation, etc.). In this context it represents the Black Buffalo of Zen's Ten Buffalo Herding drawings.

Digestion, weight gain, good appetite, sexuality, and wakefulness are all constituted in the hypothalamus. Blood pressure, heart rate, and body temperature are all influenced by it. It controls the pituitary gland and, through it, influences the whole endocrine system. It contains tiny clusters of nerve cells called nuclei that have a role in the formation of psychological and physiological states in humans and animals, such as hunger, thirst, body temperature, sexuality, sleep, joy, sadness, peace, pleasure, happiness, and other instincts, etc. It is seen as the center for expressing the worldly mind (or False Mind) through response to, and expression of, acute or unrelenting emotions, torment, emotional stress, and underlying emotions. A strong and sudden emotion such as extreme joy (as when winning the lottery) or extreme terror can all result in sudden death due to heart arrest.

However, all functions of the hypothalamus depend on our degree of awakening or delusion. If we are *deluded* and constantly follow false thoughts, we will eventually reap the consequences of pain in the body and sorrow in the mind. If we are *awakened* and practice to maintain control over our thoughts by silencing thoughts and having no mental chatter in the mind, our True Mind will emerge and our spiritual wisdom will develop. The hypothalamus will then play its role in alleviating psychosomatic illnesses and bringing about a healthy body, rosy and fresh complexion, and a blissful mind.

At the spiritual level, the hypothalamus is directly influenced by the precuneus. When the precuneus is active, the hypothalamus will immediately express a state of mind that is totally tranquil and objective. The Buddha called this state a mind that is "unified, malleable, pure, unblemished, and bright".

In summary, the hypothalamus expresses the three aspects of the human mind: the ordinary person's mind (or False Mind), the holy person's mind (or True Mind) and the Buddha-mind.

Fourth Relay Station: Precuneus

Location

The precuneus is a structure of the cerebral cortex located in the parietal lobe of both left and right hemispheres. In the division of the cerebral cortex into 52 areas by Brodmann, the precuneus is Brodmann area 7.

The precuneus relates to Ultimate Touch, Ultimate Hearing and Ultimate Wordless Awareness which are located in the external layer of the cerebral cortex.

The precuneus is situated above the cuneus which relates to Ultimate Seeing.

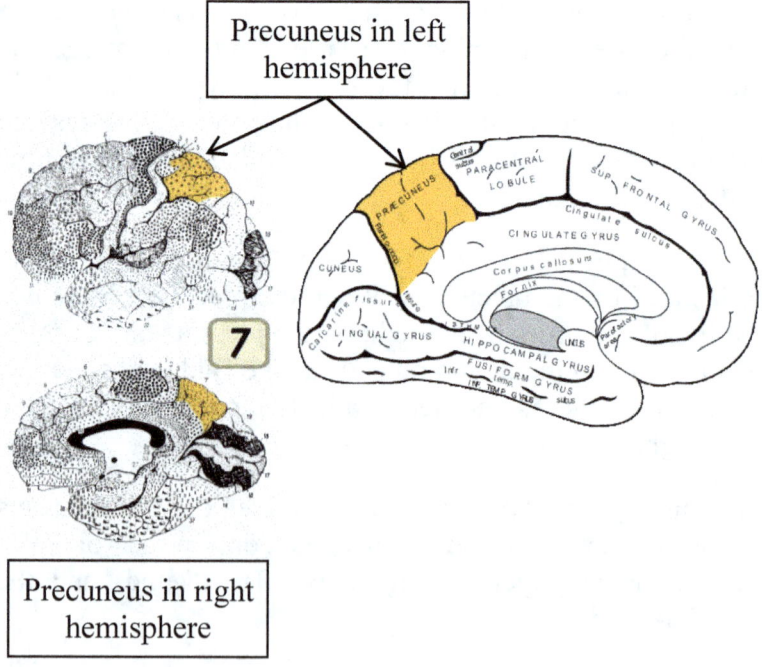

Characteristics:

- Self-cognitive awareness or more specifically, wordless self-cognitive awareness.

- Equivalent to the Suchness-Mind (or Tathā-Mind, a term used by the Buddha).

- Equivalent to Buddha-nature (Buddhatā), a term used in Developmental Buddhism.

Functions:

- Coordinates with the other three relay stations – reticular formation, thalamus and hypothalamus – to generate the default mode network of total silence of all areas deep inside the brain and in the cerebral cortex.

- Core of the brain: the precuneus is dubbed by neuroscientists the "core" of the brain due to its important role for the whole human brain.

Role:

- Take a leading role in all human activities, especially spiritual wisdom.

- Help generate harmony in body and mind.

- Develop the creative energy from within the individual human being.

- Help humans experience freedom from suffering, enlightenment, and liberation from birth and death.

Question: Master, for what reason do you call the precuneus the fourth relay station?

Answer: I call it the fourth relay station because all signals of wordless self-cognitive awareness, or wordless cognitive awareness, or wordless awake awareness are transmitted to the precuneus. They are there clearly cognized and interpreted into novel, objective, and accurate knowledge. The precuneus is the area that stores cognition maps. When we practice Zen regularly on a daily basis, after a period of time, all our experiences of samādhi (stillness of mind) or paññā (wisdom) are automatically stored in the precuneus to establish the cognition map which consists of semantic cognition, procedural cognition, episodic cognition, and evoked cognition.

Question: Master, is this fourth relay station different from the other three relay stations?

Answer: The other three relay stations – (1) reticular formation, (2) thalamus and (3) hypothalamus – have the common characteristic of receiving and transmitting *all* signals that come from outside the brain (from sensory organs and internal organs) and all signals from the brain to the peripheral nervous system and body.

On the other hand, the precuneus only receives and transmits *selected* signals, those that relate to the states of totally silent mind under wordless cognitive awareness.

Question: Master, what are other characteristics of the precuneus that the other three relay stations do not possess?

Answer: I call the precuneus the spiritual relay station because our potential for enlightenment develops from this area. We will progressively experience intuition, creativity, innovation, as well as the energy of compassion, loving-kindness, sympathetic joy, equanimity, and eloquence. These are outcomes of the process of developing our

Buddha-nature. For this reason, I call the precuneus the spiritual relay station. It is also the structure associated with Buddha-nature and potential for enlightenment innate in each human being.

The other three relay stations merely fulfill the role of objectively receiving and transmitting afferent or efferent signals. Furthermore, they do not come up with novel interpretations.

Question: The Diamond Sutra says "Anything that has an appearance is illusory". Now you say that Buddha-nature is located in the precuneus, can you please explain this point further?

Answer: The Diamond Sutra does say: "Anything that has an appearance that one can see is illusory". It is true that anything that has a form or an appearance is always changing, and this is why the sutra calls them illusory, not real. On the other hand, Buddha-nature does not have a form or appearance. However when we have a human body with a normal brain, our Buddha-nature relies on our brain to manifest its function and role. Nowadays, with modern scientific equipment, we can see that the manifestations of Buddha-nature originate in the precuneus. For this reason, I tentatively say that Buddha-nature develops from the precuneus structure in our brain.

Question: Master, and where is the Tathā-Mind located?

Answer: I have said that the precuneus has the special characteristic of being the seat of wordless cognitive awareness and self-wordless cognitive awareness, therefore we are dwelling in the precuneus when we dwell in our Tathā-Mind, for the Tathā-Mind is the mind that is "in a state of bare cognition, malleable, pure, bright, unblemished, beyond reasoning, etc.", as the Buddha described it in the suttas.

Question: Master, Zen Buddhism often says "Return home". Is this place the Tathā-Mind?

Answer: This is correct. This is the same as saying "dwelling in the precuneus".

Question: Master, could you please tell us how to practice in order to experience dwelling in the precuneus?

Answer: We gradually practice from lower levels to higher ones.

Step (1): we use single-thought awareness to tentatively quieten the mind.

Step (2): we practice wordless awareness or Silent Awareness: we will experience Ultimate Seeing, Ultimate Hearing, and Ultimate Touch.

Step (3): we practice Awake Awareness, which is clear and complete awareness without any attachment.

Step (4): we practice wordless Cognitive Awareness, or bare cognitive awareness, or self-cognitive awareness: our mind becomes totally tranquil and objective. At this point, all mental defilements, fetters, and underlying tendencies have been eliminated, and our mind becomes completely bright, pure, tranquil, and devoid of self. The Buddhist terminology for this state of mind is Tathā-Mind or Suchness-mind. The precuneus will have fulfilled its role as all structures related to language are immobile:

- The three structures Thinking Faculty, Consciousness and Intellect are immobile.

- The language pathway consisting of the Wernicke or encoding area, the Broca or decoding area, the inner talk area, and the inner dialogue area is totally immobile.

- The memory areas, consisting of working memory area, long term memory area (hippocampus), and emotional memory area (amygdala) are immobile.

- The first, second, and third relay stations are immobile.

- The anterior cingulate gyrus is immobile.

The scientific term for this state is "default mode network".

Question: Master, are there any Buddhist terms that equate to the default mode network?

Answer: Yes, there are. The Buddha called it the "No-Self" or the "Unborn". The Prajñā Pāramitā school of Buddhism called it "The Absolutely Pure and Tranquil Egoistic Self".

COMMENTARY TREATISE 7: THERAPEUTIC EFFECTS OF ZEN ON PSYCHOLOGICAL AND PSYCHOSOMATIC ILLNESSES

Therapeutic Effects of Zen on Psychological and Psychosomatic Illnesses

Practical effects of Zen

Zen has *marvelous* therapeutic effects on psychosomatic illnesses and stress.

In order to bring clarity to this topic, I will present three points: general considerations about Buddhist meditation, psychosomatic illnesses, and Zen practice to alleviate psychosomatic illnesses.

1. General considerations on Buddhist meditation

I would like to introduce the main structures in our body, the energy of which Zen aims to develop.

Introducing the Wordless Awareness Mind

When a person practices Zen using the correct teaching and technique, they will experience harmony in their body and mind, and also spiritual wisdom development, for the simple reason that in essence the practice of Zen directly impacts on the Wordless Awareness Mind areas. This is the structure that creates the *extraordinary* effects on body, mind, and spiritual wisdom development.

Wordless Awareness Mind is a Zen Buddhist term. In Early Buddhism texts, the Buddha called it the Unborn Intellect. Patriarchs of Developmental Buddhism also referred to it as the Pure Consciousness. It is *awareness without competition*. Science calls it the gnostic area or the general interpretative area, or the Wernicke Area. I call it the wordless awareness area as it corresponds to *an awareness in which there is no verbal chatter*.

For example, when we see all the objects that are in front of us very clearly and in their totality without having any verbal chatter in our mind about the objects, we are using our Wordless Awareness Mind.

The Wordless Awareness Mind is located in the rear left hemisphere of the brain. The scientific term for it is "general interpretative area" or "gnostic area". Its function is to interpret all objects of the senses without involvement of the self. Its awareness of the object is just a *silent awareness*. When it is present, sorrow, anger, worry, fear, dispute, competition, and hatred are not present. When it is present, the mind of the Zen practitioner becomes peaceful, tranquil, and serene.

Effects of the Wordless Awareness Mind

When the Wordless Awareness Mind is present, the Intellect does not get distorted, emotions are absent, and the mind becomes peaceful and serene. As a result, the body will be healthy as all physiological energies inside the body are developed uniformly. This is the effect of the Wordless Awareness Mind.

When the Wordless Awareness Mind is active, the cerebral cortex and the hypothalamus are simultaneously activated, and they in turn activate the parasympathetic nervous system and the endocrine system. A healthy body and peaceful mind are the outcomes of this chain reaction from the Wordless Awareness Mind, to the cerebral cortex, hypothalamus, pituitary gland, and endocrine glands.

This principle shows that the Wordless Awareness Mind plays an important role in the treatment or alleviation of psychosomatic illnesses. When it is present, our nerves are not tense, and worry, anger, fear, attachment, and envy are absent. There is just a *pure awareness*.

The parasympathetic nervous system is activated when the Wordless Awareness Mind is present. Its role is to release the biochemical acetylcholine which has beneficial effects on the brain and lowers blood pressure. The parasympathetic nervous system also triggers the pancreas into releasing insulin, which will help reduce diabetes progressively until the blood sugar level becomes balanced.

Practical value of Zen

In reality, the marvelous effect of Zen lies in the principle of biofeedback. Through the practice of Zen, we are able to exploit physiological energies inside our body, and as a result, lead a more meaningful life. We need to understand clearly this biofeedback principle when we practice Zen, in order to avoid incorrect practice methods that create excessive nervous tension that leads to body illnesses and more and more disturbance in the mind without us realizing it.

We can then adjust our practice method to stop any health deterioration or psychosomatic illnesses such as high blood pressure or irregular heart rate when we first notice them.

Furthermore, if we encounter people who suffer from chronic psychosomatic illnesses or stress, we will be able to guide them toward a correct meditation practice that will help them alleviate their illnesses when modern or traditional medicines are no longer effective.

Therein resides the practical value of Zen. Zen does not promise us everlasting peace and happiness in some faraway and mysterious world after we have left this body. On the contrary, Zen helps us experience right now harmony between body and mind, and real peace and joy within our surrounding environment. In our everyday life, we will have less suffering from chronic illnesses, and less stress from the dissatisfactions that life brings. We feel less worry and sorrow about the clashes that happen in everyday life. Our mind feels serenity, harmony, and amity toward everyone even though we may need to spend a lot of physical or mental energy in our work. We have an *awake awareness* in the four postures which enables us to grow the physiological energy in our body. In reality, this physiological energy consists of biochemical substances that flow inside the billions of neurons, muscle cells, endocrine system, and nervous systems, giving us our mental strength.

Brief overview of biofeedback principle

There are within the body several biochemical substances that are either beneficial or non-beneficial to the body. When we practice Zen with the correct technique, we generate a chain reaction along the axis Wordless Awareness Mind - hypothalamus - pituitary gland - endocrine glands to foster homeostasis and develop other physiological energies in the brain that make the body healthy, the mind peaceful, joyful and serene, and that help expand spiritual wisdom to a great extent. When our body is in balance, our mind feels peaceful, joyful and serene, and our memory and cognitive faculty are enhanced. This is the biofeedback principle in action.

When we practice Zen, we are applying a method to relax the mind. When the mind is relaxed, the brain and especially the hypothalamus are impacted. Biochemical substances are then released in a chain reaction, with the ultimate outcome being a healthy and alert body. The mind will immediately feel at ease, peaceful, joyful, optimistic, and in harmony with the surrounding environment. Our spiritual wisdom develops, our memory improves, and we develop a right perspective on life. Our Intellect does not get distorted.

This is the biofeedback principle in Zen. It relies on the application of correct meditation techniques to produce favorable outcomes. If we apply incorrect techniques, the result will be detrimental to the development of both body and spiritual wisdom. We may develop high blood pressure, diabetes, stomach ulcers, insomnia, despondency, a stroke, memory impairment, and declining cognition.

The human body is precious

It is serious mistake to not care for the body, let alone *abuse* it. As a Zen practitioner, we are well advised to follow the Buddha's example and consider that the body is precious. Six years of harsh self-mortification practice to oppress the body taught the Buddha the value of the body. He stopped abusing his body and saw it as a necessary vehicle that would help him attain ultimate enlightenment.

The body is the raft that helps us cross the sea of life and death. Only with a healthy body can we practice regularly. Only with a healthy body will we, while we are still living, avoid the torment of bodily disharmony such as constipation, high blood pressure, and nervous breakdown, etc. Only with a healthy body will we be able to fulfill our wish to serve humanity which should start first with members of our family. If our body is not healthy, we will not be able to practice Zen long term. When our body falls ill, we will be restricted in our practice and our mind will be affected.

Zen is an instrument that creates harmony in mankind

The important element in Zen is the development of the energy of the Wordless Awareness Mind. In reality the Wordless Awareness Mind has always been innate to us, but we don't know how to make it become an on-going presence in our life. It then becomes an energy that impacts on other structures in our brain and endocrine system. If we practice Zen using the correct method, we will be able to experience the practical value of this energy.

Nowadays, both modern medicine and psychology consider meditation as an instrument capable of treating psychosomatic illnesses and stress.

For this reason, like other sciences, Zen has been considered as an instrument for treating chronic psychosomatic illnesses and stress. Zen is also capable of helping a person live in harmony with their surrounding environment. This harmony consists of harmony between body and mind in the individual, harmony between individuals, and harmony between the individual's body and the natural climate. When body and mind are in balance, harmony will occur.

Examples:

- The Buddhist layperson, while living within their family, creates harmony between husband and wife, parents and children, and within the extended family.

Conflict, dispute, and aggression do not occur within the family.

- The Buddhist monk or nun, while living within their congregation, does not foster petty envy or dissatisfaction with other people about interest or status. Harmony, peacefulness, joy, and serenity continuously shine through every bodily action and speech.

When body and mind are in disharmony, discord will emerge. The body falls ill and the mind is disturbed. Conflict arises between individuals. Sorrow is unavoidable when body and mind are in disharmony.

The foundations of samādhi (stillness of mind) and paññā (wisdom)

Samādhi (stillness of mind) is founded upon the Wordless Awareness Mind because its characteristics are wordless awareness, absence of the False Mind, and end of dualistic thinking. What remains is referred to in the suttas as *Full and Clear Awareness*. Likewise, paññā (wisdom) is founded upon the Wordless Awareness Mind. The totality of the False Mind is located in the pre-frontal cortex of both left and right hemispheres. When the Wordless Awareness Mind is present, these areas cease to be active.

In order to apply the correct Zen techniques, we need to clearly understand the function of various areas of the cerebral cortex and limbic system, and which biochemical substances are beneficial or detrimental to the body.

For example, the role of the right pre-frontal cortex is to manifest the differentiating Consciousness. However it needs to combine with the left pre-frontal cortex to express the degree of dualistic differentiation because the inner talk area is located in the left pre-frontal cortex. The left pre-frontal cortex always expresses the functions of the False Mind, in particular the prominent role of thinking and the Intellect.

Stimulating these areas leads to psychosomatic illnesses and stress. For this reason, when a Zen practitioner experiences psychosomatic illnesses, stress, and continuous disturbance of the mind, they have been using their pre-frontal cortex during practice without realizing it while believing that they have been using the correct practice.

Conclusion

Practices that relax the mind by using single-thought awareness, wordless awareness or the higher wordless cognitive awareness all progressively lead the mind to become tranquil and serene. The Zen practitioner will be able to experience the following tangible outcomes:

- Transformation of the mind.
- Alleviation of mental and psychosomatic illnesses.
- Body and mind in balance.
- Spiritual wisdom development.

In summary, Zen will have real value to those who see it as an essential need for their body, mind, and spiritual wisdom.

Further Reading 3: Stress

Overview

In their daily life, people at all levels of culture and education, living in their worldly mind or spiritual mind, and in all occupations (from heads of state to destitute laborers, from lay to ordained practitioners) constantly have to deal with difficult, bitter, sad, painful, and terrifying situations, or live in environments that seriously threaten their life, honor, career, possession, or status, or come face to face with misfortunes, terrifying consequences, or threats to physical wellbeing such as lack of food, shelter, health, or survival, or have to concentrate to find solutions to problems. For these reasons, a person's mind is always tense and stress builds up from the challenges the person faces as the person has to mobilize all their mental capabilities and resources to think, ponder, and problem solve, and all their resources to deal with the pressure or find solutions to these serious problems.

The person who coined the term "stress"

Hans Selye (1907-1982), a Canadian endocrinologist at McGill University, Montreal, was the first person to identify in 1935 the link between stress and gastrointestinal ulcers. By injecting different hormones into mice, he observed a swelling of their adrenal cortex and atrophy of their thymus and lymphatic glands that resulted in a dysfunction of the immune system and led to gastric ulcers, duodenal inflammation and intestinal ulcers. In July 1936, he published his findings in an article entitled "A Syndrome Produced by Diverse Nocuous Agents".

In 1956, he published a book on stress entitled "The Stress of Life".

Nowadays, stress is considered the cause of many types of ulcers such as gastric ulcers.

Anger and hatred also release several acids in the stomach resulting in gastric or duodenal ulcers. (The duodenum is the first portion of the small intestine and the last portion of the stomach; it is a C-shaped structure that covers the head of the pancreas.)

Prevalence

Stress is nowadays a term commonly used in the wider population. It is considered the cause for many bodily and mental illnesses. It plays a role in the development of many mental illnesses, which in turn generate other detrimental effects on the body.

Stress is considered by modern medicine as a precursor of psycho-physiological illnesses.

For example, if a person tends to reacts with anxiety, fear, sorrow, or on-going and latent despondency to external stimuli to their seeing, hearing, and knowing, this person may potentially have stress.

Stress may also be the hidden reason for inexplicable delusions due to mental dysfunction such as an irrational fear of certain individuals that only affects the person and nobody else. Similarly, stress may be the reason for losing consciousness or turning very pale when hearing sudden bad news. This news strongly impacts on the hypothalamus, causing a sudden nervous breakdown that impacts on the sympathetic nervous system and causes it to suddenly decrease blood flow back to the heart.

Stress is an illness of our modern times that is most prevalent in developed or developing countries. This is due to the modern lifestyle that requires people to face demands that are well above the norm of centuries past. Anxiety, fear, thinking, and pondering continually operate unconsciously in people's minds.

People nowadays have to deal with many more money matters than a few centuries ago. Their body and mind are constantly tense; they need to work more than they can normally do; competition, striving, keeping up with other people, and trying to get ahead never ends; their life is already complicated and their mind even more so. The mind constantly has to withstand or deal with situations that are either serious or urgent. Consequently, systems within the body have to work harder while people don't know how to recover their energy, relax their nervous systems, or orient their mind towards tranquility even for short periods of time.

The more science and technology advance, the more people are drawn into and thrown around by these advances. If people do not know how to take control of their life – by being content with what they have – they will have great difficulty avoiding stress.

Stressors

Stress does not happen spontaneously but is the consequence of external conditions and factors that affect our mind through the senses.

There are four main categories of stressors in people's life:

1. Physical stressors

They consist of events such as:

- Changes in the weather (either too hot or too cold).

- Natural disasters (such as earthquakes, storms, floods, droughts, fires, and famines).
- Transport disasters such as road accidents, air crashes, train and ship disasters.
- Noise and animation in cities, neighborhood or overcrowding.
- Concentration camps and reeducation prison camps.
- Air pollution.
- Unsafe areas.
- War zones, traumas caused by wars and armed conflicts.

2. Biological stressors

They consist of inferiority complexes caused by:

- The body is not in balance, abnormal, deteriorated, weak, or having an abnormal constitution.
- Having incurable chronic illnesses.
- Looking every day in the mirror to check facial complexion, hair style, body shape, and clothing appearance is also a fundamental cause of stress at all ages.

Excessive mental arousal is another stressor, but one that is not often identified as such. Arousal is an important function of the mind that plays an important role in the resolution of ordinary or serious problems. Without arousal, we do not pay attention to what is happening around us and are not able to see details. Perception, memory, attention, and emotions all require arousal. However, if we focus our arousal too much on an object, our nervous system becomes tense and anxiety starts to arise. Stress will then follow.

3. *Social stressors*

They correspond to the following situations:

- Loss of job or unemployment.
- Death of wife, husband, or partner.
- Loss of a dear relative or dear friend.
- Status or reputation ruined.
- Loss of, or threat to, power.
- Change in employment.
- High cost of housing.
- Too much debt.
- Difficulty in love relationship.
- Children leaving home.
- Change in living conditions.
- Terrifying or sorrowful memories of war or refugee displacement.
- Divorce or separation.
- Imprisonment.

- Traumatic memories.

- Complex problems with boss or employer.

- Homelessness, loneliness, and poverty.

- Demands, needs, opportunities, and goals not compatible with desires or wishes, etc.

These causes lead to:

- Unending internal conflicts, sudden nervous breakdown, inhibited or suppressed emotions, feeling pressured from all sides, traumas, panic attack, disappointment, and anxiety.

Anxiety is an emotion that is similar to fear. It is however different from fear because anxiety has no reason or purpose, whereas fear has reasons and purposes. Anxiety is very vague. It consists of expecting an unpredictable and ill-defined danger while in a sorrowful state of mind. Anxiety leads to nervous tension, repeated anxiety becomes chronic. Anxiety is a cause for stress.

4. Psychological stressors

They correspond to the following situations:

- Strong and enduring emotions, such as remorse (due to committing serious sins).

- Haunting memories and nightmares.

- Anger and hatred.

- Fear.

- Despair.

- Profound despondency.
- Fear of death when in old age.
- Even excessive joy can also lead to stress.

Inferiority complexes due to social conditions such as poverty, privation, lack of intelligence, feeling guilty, or loneliness in old age (having no support from children or society) also lead to chronic stress.

Furthermore, stress can be caused by situations of competition or striving to obtain something important in life, or being pressured to do something on a regular basis. People subjected to these situations constantly live under pressure, in a hurry, and with high mental tension.

Action and effect

Stress is generated as a response to external stimuli such as anger, hatred, grief, enduring despondency, or imagined reasons for anxiety and fear. It is formed by activities of the brain that involve the cerebral cortex, hypothalamus, endocrine system, and sympathetic nervous system.

Stress results in the release of the hormone cortisol from the adrenal cortex and epinephrine from the adrenal medulla. These hormones alter the heart rate, blood pressure, and metabolism.

Cortisol is one of the hormones released by the adrenal cortex depending on the level of stress. A moderate level of cortisol is not harmful to the organism and may even be beneficial as it strengthens the immune system. However, when it is released excessively day after day to the point of becoming chronic, it becomes a poison to the brain. When cortisol follows the blood stream to reach the brain, it constricts receptors in the cytoplasm of many neurons. It kills or damages millions of neurons in the long term memory area (hippocampus) resulting in memory loss. A high level of cortisol in the cerebral cortex is a cause for Alzheimer's disease. It results in an atrophy of the parietal, temporal, and occipital lobes which form the general interpretative area. It is also a cause for reduced blood flow into the brain, starving neurons of oxygen.

Stress becomes chronic when we are regularly under stress. The brain will then get damaged.

Epinephrine increases the heart rate and blood sugar level, constricts blood vessels (resulting in increased blood pressure and heart rate), and redirects blood flows toward the brain, heart and skeletal muscles.

At the same time, the sympathetic nervous system is activated, resulting in increased heart rate, quickened breathing, increased blood sugar level, constriction of peripheral blood vessels, inhibited digestion, as well as other effects on the body.

Chronic stress leads to high blood pressure, which causes damage to the heart, blood vessels and kidneys (a blood pressure reading of 140/90 is considered high).

People under chronic stress are prone to cardiovascular diseases and damage to the heart, which lead to heart attack and death.

Psycho-physiological illnesses such as high blood pressure, ulcers and migraines are not caused by physical dysfunctions. Resentment, anger, hatred, and anxiety stimulate the production of digestive acids that cause ulcers in the wall of the stomach and small intestines.

Grief and depression that follow the death of a life partner weaken the immune system and increase the risk of a stroke or heart attack.

Stress weakens the immune system.

Emotions and depression are linked to cancers.

Definitions

If we consider symptoms, stress can be defined as:

- The expression of a psychological state of agitation, tenseness, imbalance, or disparity between the perceived demands and needs of an urgent situation the individual is facing and their ability to resolve it.
- Or a state of intense emotional reaction or psychological tension, or feeling pressured from all sides, or excessive emotional engagement in a topic, or a relived trauma from past memories. The severity of the stress depends on the reaction from the individual's intellect or cognition, or their own perspective.

Example 1

Anxiety, insomnia, depression, or severe despair generated by witnessing an event that increases fear or terror, such as the death of a loved one, divorce or separation, birth of a child, loneliness in a foreign land, or situations of terror and destruction of war, etc.

Example 2

Stress generated by constantly exercising the Consciousness or Intellect to focus attention on a topic of meditation, or by using awake consciousness or excessive arousal when practicing meditation.

If we consider effects, stress can be defined as:

- A psychological illness that may lead to ulcers in internal organs such as gastric ulcers, intestinal ulcers, or even cancers. The various stressors mentioned previously impact on the brain and in particular the hypothalamus. A series of physiological reactions inside the body follow, such as the release of biochemical substances in the adrenal glands and sympathetic nervous system, which ultimately lead to damage to internal organs and the brain. For this reason, stress is considered a cause of mental and physical illness and has been dubbed a "psycho-physiological illness".

The effects of stress on the body are illnesses such as gastric ulcers, intestinal ulcers, high blood pressure, cardio vascular diseases, coronary heart diseases, myocardial infarction, heart attack, stroke, hemiplegia, diabetes, cancer, and brain damage, etc.

The effects of stress on the mind are illnesses such as depression, memory loss, etc.

In summary, stress is a complex reaction of the mind to on-going tension that arises from a mental problem, an event, or the environment that the individual is facing or has to resolve. It affects everyone, young and old, lay people and members of the sangha. While dealing with the problem, the nervous system becomes tense, mental states are manifested according to each situation, and biochemical substances are released within the body in accordance with reactions of the mind.

This psychological pressure results in psychosomatic illnesses.

Dealing with stress

Zen can help alleviate stress in several ways:

Relaxing the mind or relaxing thoughts is an important part of the biofeedback principle in Zen. It is the antidote to stress. Sitting relaxed in meditation strengthens the immune system, and lowers blood pressure, heart rate, and oxygen consumption.

1. Two-pace breathing: silently aware of breathing in, silently aware of breathing out.
2. Not naming objects.
3. Not labeling objects.
4. Bare attention.
5. Seeing, hearing, sensing things as they are.
6. Internalizing suchness or dwelling in the Tathā-Mind.
7. Internalizing Emptiness Samādhi.

Stress adaptation syndrome

The stress adaptation syndrome consists of three stages: (1) alarm stage, (2) resistance stage, and (3) exhaustion stage.

The body's first reaction to stress is an **alarm reaction**. A signal is sent to the hypothalamus which releases CRH (corticotropin-releasing hormones). CRH impacts on two systems:

1. The anterior pituitary which releases ACTH (adrenocorticotropic hormone). ACTH follows the blood stream to reach the adrenal cortex and triggers it into releasing glucocorticoid hormones that have the effect of increasing the blood sugar level.

2. The sympathetic nervous system, which is one of the two branches of the autonomic nervous system.

The sympathetic nervous system, once activated, increases heart rate, quickens breathing, increases blood sugar level, constricts peripheral blood vessels, and stops digestion, as well as having other effects. The sympathetic nervous system also triggers the adrenal medulla into releasing epinephrine (adrenaline) and norepinephrine (noradrenaline).

The alarm reaction lasts just a few minutes, depending on the duration of the stressor, with a few hours being a maximum. When the stress ends, the parasympathetic nervous system takes its place and the body begins the recovery process.

However, this is not the end for all stresses. If the stress continues, the body enters the second stage or **resistance stage.** During this stage, the body starts to activate the hypothalamus-pituitary gland-adrenal cortex axis.

During the resistance stage, the pituitary gland, under activation by the hypothalamus, releases the hormone ACTH (adrenocorticotrophic hormone). ACTH acts on the adrenal cortex, which releases the glucocorticoid, hydrocortisone, corticosterone and cortisol hormones. These hormones fulfill different functions. They help the autonomic nervous system maintain epinephrine and norepinephrine. They stimulate the conversion of fat and protein into glucose, in particular the conversion of glycogen stored in the liver, with the result being an increase in energy for the organism.

Exhaustion stage: this stage only develops if stress has reached an extremely serious level. If stress continues to rise, the hormone cortisol is released. The body is not able to cope with the stressor, and death may occur.

The person experiences strong emotional intensity and several physical symptoms such as muscle tightness, shortness of breath, and nervous overstimulation symptoms such as tingles, stomach churns, and insomnia. Hemiplegia (paralysis of half of the body) may occur, caused by venous inflammation (phlebitis) that results in blood clots.

Psychological and physical factors interact with each other in a complex manner to shape physical health.

Both epinephrine and norepinephrine stimulate the heart and constrict blood vessels in the skin and internal organs. Norepinephrine constricts blood vessels and increases blood pressure more. Epinephrine released by the adrenal medulla increases the heart rate, constricts blood vessels while expanding coronary and skeletal muscle arteries, increases blood pressure and blood sugar levels, inhibits smooth muscles in the bronchioles and intestines, and dilates pupils.

Social pressures about people's position in society push them to increase their mental activities, eventually leading to coronary heart disease.

Stress has detrimental health effects. It has links with asthma, arthritis, cancer, diabetes, heart disease, and psychosomatic disorders that lead to ulcers.

It has an impact on all sorts of programs and plans, and on creativity.

Hardening of the arteries (arteriosclerosis) is caused by the buildup of lipid (cholesterol) plaques inside large arteries. People with clogged coronary arteries may suffer from angina and heart attack.

Stress is known to play a role in the hardening of arteries. Activated by the sympathetic nervous system, the adrenal cortex releases epinephrine and norepinephrine. Excessive levels of these two substances result in lipid buildup on the wall of arteries.

Stress caused by the loss of a loved one leads to disorders in the endocrine system. The result is a heightened risk of coronary heart disease.

Role of the hypothalamus in relation to stress

The hypothalamus, a structure located under the thalamus, has centers that regulate satiety, thirst, sexual activities, sleep, and body temperature. It also plays a role in mediating emotional states such as rage, terror, and pleasure.

In regards to stress, the hypothalamus plays the role of coordinator and integrator of nervous system activities.

1. The sympathetic nervous system and adrenal glands (in which the adrenal medulla secretes epinephrine and norepinephrine) is especially important in the fight or flight response or when the organism is committed to a response action. Responses from the cardio vascular system, breathing, endocrine system, and other systems are aimed at ensuring that the body has sufficient energy to address the problem.

2. The axis hypothalamus-pituitary gland-adrenal glands come into play when the organism is faced with chronic stress or is unable to respond to stressors. For example, a person works with a difficult boss and has to silently put up with unpleasant and bombastic comments on a daily basis. These comments are stressors for the person, whose intellect comes into play to find a way to deal with the attitude of the boss. Inside the brain, the hypothalamus stimulates the pituitary gland into releasing ACTH into the blood stream, which in turn stimulates the adrenal cortex into releasing steroid hormones that are rich in fat. The body increases attention on the attitude of the boss and the sympathetic nervous system is activated. Heart rate decreases and body movement is inhibited.

Stages of stress adaptation

In 1976, Hans Selye, a Canadian physiologist published a three-stage model of reaction to stress that he called the General Adaptation Syndrome: 1) Alarm reaction, 2) Resistance reaction, and 3) Exhaustion reaction.

Stage 1: Alarm reaction

This is the stage of response to the stress. Stress starts when something is identified as a threat or something that needs to be fought off. Emotions rise and activate the sympathetic nervous system-adrenal medulla complex. A "red alert light" is switched on. The organism becomes alert and vigilant. The breath quickens, heart rate increases, muscles tense up, and changes to increase body strength occur. These changes enable the organism to mobilize resources to regain self-control. Nerve signals light up in the sympathetic nervous system, resulting in the secretion of epinephrine into the blood stream. Immediately, the heart rate increases, breathing quickens, blood pressure increases, and blood-flows to the skin, digestive system, and excretory system stop. At this stage, the individual has to use defense mechanisms. If the stress cannot be reduced, one enters the adaptation stage.

Stage 2: Resistance reaction

Bodily symptoms and other signs of tension appear as if the organism is fighting the increased psychological disturbance. If we are successful in reducing the stress, the body returns to a more normal state. However, if the stress reaches excessive levels or continues, we may become desperate. When this happens, bodily and emotional energy depletion and signs of decline become more apparent.

Stage 3: Exhaustion reaction

If the stress continues for too long, the organism may reach the third stage which is exhaustion. This is the final stage. The pituitary and adrenal glands reach their limits and no longer have the energy to fulfill their functions. Finally, the body becomes exhausted and all alert reactions become ineffective. For this reason, chronic stress always leads to death.

The brain and body are physical elements while the mind consists of thoughts and emotions. They are all subject to the four laws of impermanence, conflict, insubstantiality and dependent origination or cause and effect.

Only humans feel love, hate, disappointment, passion, optimism, pessimism, emotions and reason. What structure expresses the states of the mind? It is the brain, or more fundamentally the brain cells.

Body and mind always interact with each other. The mind affects the body, and vice versa, the body affects the mind.

With Zen, body and mind are in harmony. The Zen practitioner needs to follow appropriate principles that Zen has stipulated.

The peripheral nervous system and emotions

Sensory receptors in the five sense organs (eyes, ears, nose, tongue and skin) provide information about the external world. Receptors in skeletal muscles and joints provide information about the body's posture, position, orientation and movement. Receptors in smooth muscles and internal organs provide feedback on what is happening inside the body: feelings of hunger, thirst, nausea and internal sensations. All this information is transmitted to the Central Nervous System through afferent pathways.

On the other hand, efferent nervous impulses bring information from the Central Nervous System to the Peripheral Nervous System. They allow the brain to affect muscles, organs and glands. These efferent pathways are also called centrifugal or motor pathways.

The brain is able to use information coming from both the body and internal organs to form emotional judgments. Receptors in skeletal muscles and joints (such as in the face, hands or feet) send signals to the brain through the somatic afferent nerves. Receptors in smooth muscles and internal organs (such as stomach and intestines) send signals to the brain through visceral afferent nerves. Through these means, the brain receives information about facial muscle movements, internal organ activities, position of the limbs, and internal distress, etc. From this information, expressions are manifested such as knitting brows, clenching teeth, stomach ache, or cold neck.

The peripheral nervous system consists of two main branches: the autonomic nervous system and the somatic nervous system. The somatic nervous system consists of neurons connecting the brain to and from sensory organs and motor organs (such as skeletal muscles). The autonomic nervous system consists of brain neurons that regulate smooth muscles, the heart muscle and glands. Autonomic means "self-governing". The autonomic nervous system innervates the cardiovascular system, respiratory system, digestive system and endocrine system which consists of the adrenal glands, testes and ovaries. The autonomic nervous system is especially important in the expression of emotions.

It is called "autonomic" because it operates mainly outside conscious control. While we can consciously control our skeletal muscles, we cannot easily direct our smooth muscles and heart muscle. This latter is done by the autonomic nervous system.

Stressors

Depending on the cultural or traditional context, stressors can originate from the following situations:

1. Unemployment. This is a key source of stressors.
2. Death of a husband, wife or partner.
3. Bereavement.
4. Separation and divorce.
5. Anxiety.

6. Loneliness.

7. Imprisonment.

8. Death of a close family member.

9. Unfulfilled marriage or love.

10. Chronic illness.

11. Abuse.

12. Unmet expectations.

13. Fighting in a war.

14. Traumatic experience.

15. Natural catastrophes: storm, flood, earthquake, fire, air crashes.

Conclusion

Stress is an illness of the 20th century and our modern times. Whether they live in an under-developed or developed country, people have to face many difficult situations in their daily life. If we do not know how to regulate our mind and body to adapt to our family, work, societal and natural environment, we may suffer serious consequences such as stress, followed by other psychosomatic illnesses.

The antidote to all psychological and psychosomatic illnesses is the Zen method taught by Sakkamuni Buddha. The essence of Zen is always living in wordless awareness (called Right Awareness in the suttas), knowing everything clearly without being attached (called Full and Clear Awareness in the suttas) and wordless cognitive awareness.

From this foundation we will experience harmony in our body and mind, and the development of our spiritual wisdom.

Further Reading 4: Psychosomatic Illnesses

Definitions

The term "psychosomatic" is a combination of two Greek words: "psyche" meaning *mind* and "soma" meaning *body*. "Psychosoma" means a dysfunction of the mind that causes an illness in the body, mainly affecting an internal organ. Modern psychologists use the term "psychosomatic diseases" or "psychosomatic illnesses" in these circumstances. For example, emotions such as anxiety, fear, anger, hatred, despair, jealousy, or excessive joy cause illnesses such as high blood pressure, gastric ulcers, migraine pain on one side of the head, asthma, diabetes, heart attack, etc., which are not caused by a dysfunction in the body.

Chain reaction

In reality, emotions and underlying tendencies – which are those sorrows that are smoldering inside the mind – continually impact on the brain and particularly the hypothalamus. From there, nerve impulses are transmitted to the sympathetic nervous system. A chain reaction occurs resulting in the release of biochemical substances from the sympathetic nervous system and the endocrine system. These biochemical substances cause illness to the body. Therefore, psychosomatic illnesses are illnesses of the body caused by repeated emotions exerted on the mind.

Using Zen's terminology, the cause is an excessive disturbance of the False Mind. The disturbance signal then impacts on the hypothalamus, which activates the sympathetic system and then the endocrine system, leading to illness in the body.

The root cause of psychosomatic illnesses is the contact between sensory organs and external objects, which cause the False Mind to get excessively disturbed and give rise to excessive anxiety, fear or effort. These disturbances impact on the hypothalamus which triggers chemical reactions in the sympathetic nervous system and endocrine system.

Inside the family and out in society, people continually have to face difficult, distressing, sad, painful or terrifying situations, or are under pressure coming from all sides, or have to deal with serious threats to their life, honor, career, possession or status. These situations lead to excessive nervous tension and result in psychosomatic illnesses.

Causes for psychosomatic illnesses or stress:

- In our role as head of family or head of enterprise, we have to deal with serious money matters such as monthly payment of debts and bills for housing, vehicle, equipment, wages, business premises, etc. We may also carry too much debt. We are always anxious because we need to deal with monthly expenses.

- If we continually live in an environment where there is a threat to our life, health, possession, honor, status, interest or power, we will develop excessive confusion, anxiety and fear.

- Having to continually deal with difficult, distressing, sad, death-related or terrifying situations.

- Coming face to face with misfortunes in life such as poverty, hunger, natural catastrophes, or accidents causing death to loved ones.

- Losing all hope in life, leading to despair and loss of interest in the external world.

- Disappointment from something in which we have put all our trust.

- Sudden strong emotions such as excessive joy, excessive terror, excessive fear or excessive anger resulting in extreme nervous tension.

- Obsessed by fear of misfortune befalling ourselves or our family, or obsessed by sad memories.

- Long term unemployment, trying hard to find a job without success.

- Psychological trauma caused by images of the terrifying death of relatives or friends in war or in some horrible accident.

- Exerting too much effort, or exerting effort for too long, or using too much vigor or too much arousal to concentrate the mind in the practice of meditation, continuing to exert effort when the point of nervous tension has been reached.

Conclusion

The cause for psychosomatic illnesses is essentially any hidden and ongoing emotions or sorrows that have reached an excessive level.

Explaining worry and anxiety

Worrying about something is a normal thing in daily life. Whatever we do in our daily life, we have some lower or higher level of worry or anxiety, even if we have understood the laws of impermanence, conflict (or suffering) and insubstantiality (or no-self) that apply to all worldly phenomena in the universe.

We cannot avoid worry and anxiety because, as commonly said, we are just normal people and are not machines or saints; we have not attained enlightenment; we are yet to reach the end of the spiritual path; we have not gained the capability, through practice, of keeping our emotions under control; or we have not internalized the higher Buddhist samādhi levels.

Worry and anxiety

Worry is feeling disquiet about something and having to focus the mind on it, but without reaching the level of causing bewilderment, fear, or psychosomatic illnesses.

On the other hand, anxiety or nervousness is a state of disquiet of the mind that is enduring. Emotions arise as a result of anxiety. Anxiety is similar to fear, yet different. When we are anxious, we continually picture or imagine some danger that will befall ourselves or our family. Anxiety does not have any tangible basis, whereas fear has basis and objectives. Anxiety is very vague but can generate fear, terror, confusion, and suffering.

Anxious states of mind

Examples:

- Feeling anxious about our impending death, being poor and destitute, being lonely in old age, possible biological warfare, the end of the world, etc.

In monastic life, there is also anxiety. Each person has different anxieties depending on their position and responsibilities.

Some anxieties take extreme forms, while others are latent and incremental. The latter form is close to what is called *underlying tendencies* in Buddhism. The mind is smoldering with latent anxiety. Under this form of anxiety, the mind is always tense and eventually stress develops. Stress is a high intensity emotional reaction and psychological tension caused by pressure coming from many sides or mental traumas that keep being recalled from memory.

Effects of anxiety

If anxiety becomes chronic, its latent character causes the sympathetic nervous system to be strongly activated. As a result, cortisol and epinephrine are released in high quantity from the adrenal cortex and adrenal medulla respectively. These two hormones cause an increase in the heart rate, blood sugar levels, and blood pressure leading to psychosomatic illnesses. As the sympathetic nervous system is activated, peripheral blood vessels are constricted, and digestion stopped. From the nerve endings of the sympathetic nervous system, a biochemical substance called norepinephrine is released. Norepinephrine follows the blood stream to reach the adrenal medulla, causing more norepinephrine and epinephrine to be released into the blood stream. The result is quickened heart rate, quickened breathing, higher blood pressure, and a disturbed mind.

Effects of norepinephrine and epinephrine

When a person is angry, their sympathetic nervous system is also activated. It releases *norepinephrine* that causes the person to become violent and aggressive, wanting to fight and destroy. For people who are prone to fear, *epinephrine* causes them to turn skittish and wanting to flee. These two substances consist of fat and they increase the fat level in the blood. Increases in blood cholesterol are partly caused by them. Epinephrine also reduces the liver's ability to retain glucose, which is released into the blood stream causing an increase in blood sugar levels.

Furthermore, when the mind is disturbed or permanently tense, signals are sent to the hypothalamus.

When the hypothalamus receives a signal of anxiety or fear, it activates the pituitary gland with a hormone called corticotropin-releasing hormone or CRH. The pituitary gland then releases the adrenocorticotrophic hormone or ACTH that actions directly on the adrenal cortex. ACTH is also released when a person is despondent or depressed. It causes the adrenal cortex to release *cortisol*.

Cortisol is a hormone that is released by the adrenal cortex depending on the degree of nervous tension. A moderate level of cortisol is not harmful to the organism and can even be beneficial as it strengthens the immune system. However, when cortisol is released in excess day after day and becomes chronically high, it becomes a poison to the brain. When it follows the blood stream into the brain, it causes neurons to be wrapped tightly and strangulated. In particular, it can kill or damage millions of neurons in the long term memory area (the hippocampus), resulting in loss of memory and cognitive function. Alzheimer's disease, with its memory degradation in old age, may be caused in part by a high level of cortisol in the cerebral cortex. Cortisol causes the cerebral cortex in the parietal, temporal and occipital lobes to shrink, resulting in a weakened constitution and impacting on arms, legs, face, head, movement, and speech. An example of a symptom is not being able to name an object, and only remembering its name after a while. Cortisol also causes a reduction in blood flow to the brain, thus starving brain cells of oxygen, and causing fatigue and dizziness.

A high level of cortisol also inhibits the formation of antibodies, causing the organism to be prone to infections.

Types of psychosomatic illnesses

- Anxiety, fear, or striving hard in meditation practice, mental or physical work will lead to illnesses of the body such as:

Migraine (pain on one side of the head), asthma, gastric ulcer, kidney disorder, irregular heartbeat, mental disorder, nervous breakdown, coronary heart disease, Parkinson's disease, high blood pressure, despondency or depression, arthritis, intestinal ulcer, diabetes, sudden heart failure causing death, suicide, or dementia.

Further explanation on Parkinson's disease

Parkinson's disease is a degenerative disorder of the brain (or nervous system), caused by a lack of *dopamine* in the brain and resulting in ailments of the body such as: muscle stiffness, movement impairment, unsteady walk, shuffling gait, body bending forward, stiff posture, inability to straighten arms, hand shaking, heavy head, unexpressive face as if wearing a heavy mask, and speech impairment. In a healthy person, dopamine is produced in the substantia nigra, a brain structure located in the brain stem. It then goes through the hypothalamus and propagates through blood vessels to the whole cerebral cortex.

Further explanation on depression

Depression means loss of all hope, enthusiasm for work, or interest in anything. It causes feelings of sadness, despondency, melancholy, loss of all hope in the future, loss of enthusiasm, loss of energy for work, thoughts of death, and suicide. Vegetative symptoms of depression include sleep disorder, such as insomnia or too much sleep, loss of appetite, weight loss, constipation, and loss of sexual drive.

Effects of meditation

We can alleviate psychosomatic illnesses by practicing Zen. Psychosomatic illnesses are caused by disturbances of the mind such as anxiety, fear, stress, anger, resentment, sadness, or on-going depression. Alleviating disturbances of the mind is precisely the primary objective of Zen. Zen has the ability to relax the mind, bringing it serenity, high-spiritedness, and peacefulness.

Important role in biofeedback principle

Relaxation is an important condition in the biofeedback principle. It is the antidote to stress in particular, and to all emotional disturbances and nervous system dysfunction in general. More important, it helps prevent or treat psychosomatic illnesses by directly impacting on the parasympathetic nervous system and the cerebral cortex.

When the mind is silent, dopamine is released by the brain stem. Dopamine has the ability to bring health to the body and treat Parkinson's disease.

When the parasympathetic nervous system is activated, the neurotransmitter *acetylcholine* is released by cells in the motor cortex, hypothalamus and brain stem. Acetylcholine neutralizes the effects of epinephrine and norepinephrine.

Acetylcholine also plays an important role in learning, memory formation, cognitive function development and helps keep the body active, i.e. the limbs can move easily. Alzheimer's disease sufferers especially lack acetylcholine.

For these reasons, acetylcholine plays a very important role. It helps us maintain wakefulness and improve memory. Many areas of the brain as well as the reticular formation in the brain stem contain acetylcholine.

Practice method

As the mind becomes serene, all emotions stop and activities of the sympathetic nervous system and adrenal glands reduce. Acetylcholine stops epinephrine and norepinephrine from being released. The heart rate decreases, blood pressure comes back to normal, and muscles relax. By generating a feeling of high-spiritedness, acetylcholine eliminates depression. It causes ACTH to decrease, thus decreasing cortisol. It also gives us greater enthusiasm for work.

Conclusion

As we realize that illnesses of the body originate in disturbances of the mind, we can apply Zen's methods of bringing the mind under control to prevent or treat our illnesses. When we apply methods to bring the mind under control, we are actually using our *awakened Intellect* to conduct our practice. The essence of this practice requires us to relax our mind or relax our thoughts. Once we achieve this relaxation of mind and relaxation of thoughts, we will be able to alleviate and treat psychosomatic illnesses. This is the process of developing wordless awareness, Silent Awareness, wordless Awake Awareness, and wordless Cognitive Awareness.

COMMENTARY TREATISE 8:

RESULTS OF EXPERIMENTS PERFORMED ON MASTER REVEREND THÍCH THÔNG TRIỆT

Results of Experiments Performed on Master Reverend Thích Thông Triệt

by Dr. Michael Erb

The last measurements of Master Reverend Thích Thông Triệt were performed on 8th and 9th of June 2013. Here I report some of the results from these experiments, combining functional magnetic resonance imaging (f-MRI) with simultaneous high density electroencephalography (EEG, 256 channels).

RESULTS OF EXPERIMENTS 213

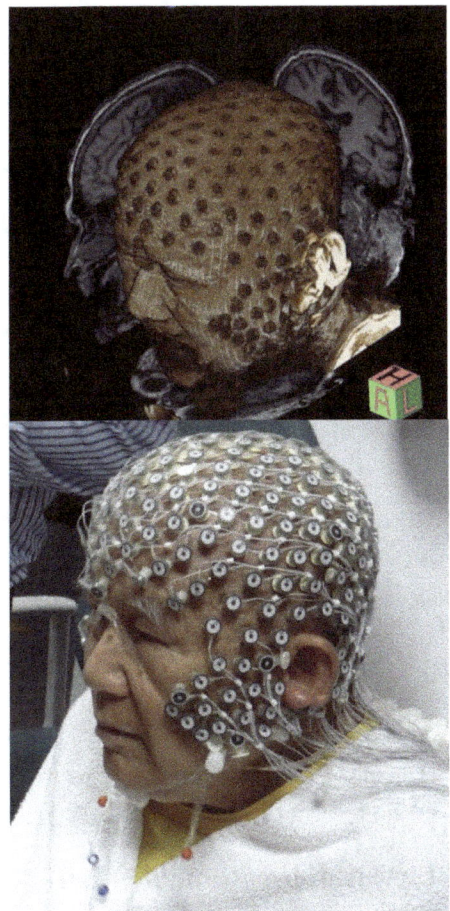

Figure 1: Magnetic Resonance Imaging (MRI, top) and high density electroencephalography (EEG). As there were still problems with the evaluation of the combined EEG (Figure, bottom), I concentrate in the following on the fMRI results.

Problem with EEG Evaluation

• Still Artifacts (bad contact) after correction (condition breathing)

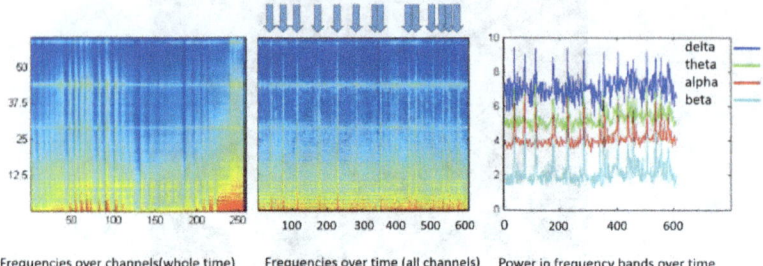

Frequencies over channels(whole time) | Frequencies over time (all channels) | Power in frequency bands over time

Figure 2: Residual artifacts in the EEG data

In the different tasks, two types of paradigm have been used, the block design with altering between two different conditions (e.g. a meditation condition and a control condition of "day-to-day thinking") and runs with continuous task over the whole measurement period. According to this, we used different data evaluation methods showing the difference between activation levels (t-maps) or difference between network connectivity (ECM, Lohmann 2010) based on correlation analysis.

12.1 Different levels of breathing meditation

Meditation means to recognize the nature of mind, the pure awareness on top of which the thoughts arise like waves on the ocean. To reach this state, the Buddha has introduced a method, which consists of observing one's own breathing. In the first stage, one has to say silently (inner speech) "I know that I breathe in, I know that I breathe out." In the second stage, the inner speech is omitted and a thought of tacit awareness is practiced. The third stage leads to a thought of awakening awareness.

RESULTS OF EXPERIMENTS

In this experiment, Master Thích Thông Triệt was asked to practice stage 1 in the first 2 minutes of a 10 minutes fMRI measurement, followed by 4 minutes of stage 2 and 4 minutes of stage 3. In order to find out in which way the cooperation between the four relay stations of the brain was changed, we calculated the mean time course of the fMRI signal in the four Regions Of Interest (ROIs, Figure 3): reticular formation (Formatio ret), thalamus (Thal), hypothalamus (Hypothal), and precuneus (Prec).

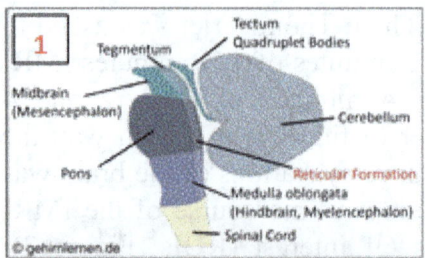
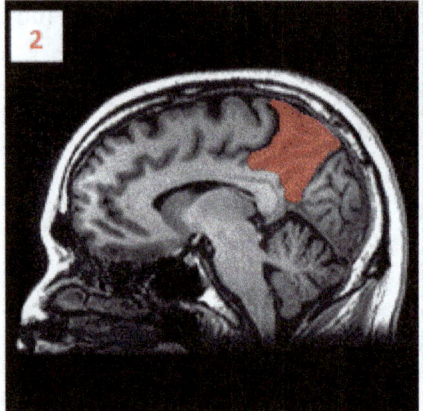

Figure 3: Position of the Four relay stations in the brain:

- Reticular Formation (No. 1),
- Thalamus and Hypothalamus (No. 3),
- Precuneus (No. 2, 4).

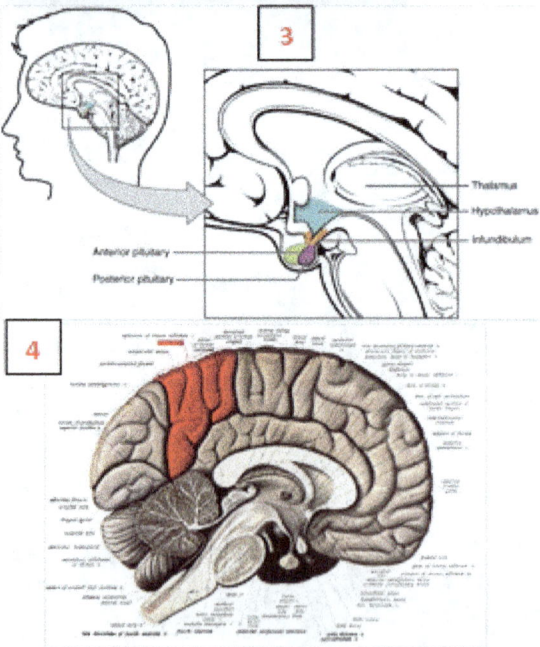

RESULTS OF EXPERIMENTS 217

Analysis in the three stages (blue, green, red) resulted in the following correlation values between the ROIs (Figure 4).

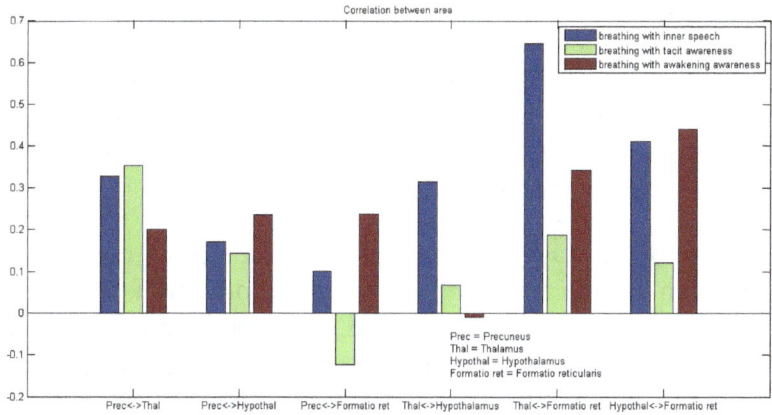

Figure 4: Correlation between the four relay stations of the brain (precuneus, thalamus, hypothalamus, and reticular formation) in the three stages of breathing meditation.

The correlation between the precuneus and the thalamus was reduced in the third state ("awakening awareness"[1]). In contrast to this, the correlation between the precuneus and the hypothalamus was increased.

In the second stage, breathing with "tacit awareness"[2], the activity in the precuneus was changing in opposite direction compared to the activity in the reticular formation (negative correlation) whereas in the third stage the correlation was again positive.

The correlation between the thalamus and the hypothalamus was high only in the first stage (breathing with inner

---

[1] Also referred to in this book as "awake awareness".
[2] Also referred to in this book as "silent awareness".

speech) and disappeared in the third stage ("awakening awareness").

Looking at the correlation between the thalamus and the reticular formation, we found a high positive value in the first stage (breathing with inner speech), a reduced value in the second stage, and again a high value in the third stage. The same pattern was found in the correlation between the hypothalamus and the reticular formation.

So the first stage is dominated by a strong correlation between the thalamus and the reticular formation (0.65) and a little less correlation between the hypothalamus and the reticular formation (0.41) and between the hypothalamus and the thalamus (0.31). The correlation between the precuneus and the other relay stations is decreasing from the thalamus (0.33), the hypothalamus (0.17) to the reticular formation (0.1).

The decreasing of the correlation between the precuneus and the other relay stations was even stronger in the second stage (0.35, 0.14, and -1.2). The correlations between the reticular formation and the thalamus (0.19) and the hypothalamus (0.12) respectively were much lower than in stage 1. In addition, the correlation between the hypothalamus and the thalamus (0.07) was considerably reduced.

In the third state, the correlation between the precuneus and the other relay stations was more or less equal (0.20, 0.24, and 0.24). The correlations between the reticular formation and the thalamus (0.34) and hypothalamus (0.44) respectively were again increased compared to stage 2. The correlation between the hypothalamus and the thalamus (-0.01) completely disappeared.

12.2 Bare Cognitive Awareness

In the next measurement session, Master Thích Thông Triệt was asked to practice "Bare Cognitive Awareness" (Nhận Thức Biết Trống Rỗng), the next level of meditation for 10 minutes. We used the calculation of eigenvector centrality maps (ECM) as described in Lohmann et. al. (2010) to analyze this session and compared it to the mean over all sessions. Eigenvector centrality attributes a value to each voxel in the brain such that a voxel receives a large value if it is strongly correlated with many other nodes that are themselves central within the network.

This method does not require a parceling into ROIs but can be calculated on a voxel-wise level.

The highest increase of connectivity in "Cognitive Awareness" compared to the mean of all other sessions (shown in red in Figure 5) was found in the left Heschl's gyrus (BA 41, BA 42, BA 22). Decreased connectivity (shown in green or blue in Figure 5) was found in the left superior temporal gyrus (BA 22/BA 39).

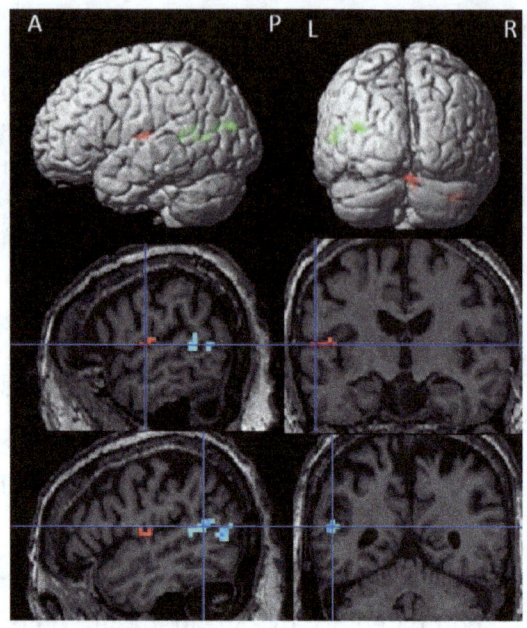

Figure 5: Different network connection in the session "Cognitive Awareness" Upper row: Brain surface from left and back; Middle row: sagittal and coronal plane in the left Heschl's gyrus (BA 41, BA 42, BA 22); Lower row: sagittal and coronal plane in the left superior temporal gyrus (BA 22/BA 39). Increased connectivity (ECM) in "Cognitive Awareness" compared to the mean of all sessions is shown in red, decreased connectivity is shown in green or blue.

RESULTS OF EXPERIMENTS

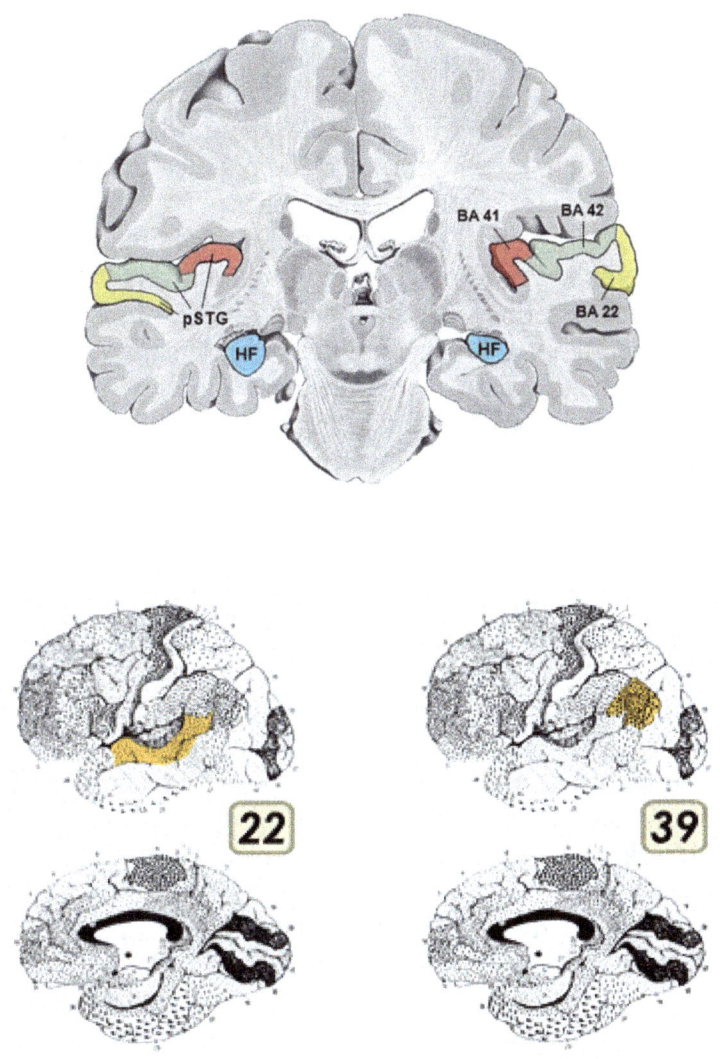

Figure 6: Schematic position of the Heschl's gyri (BA 41, BA 42, BA 22), left middle temporal gyrus (BA 22), and left angular gyrus (BA 39).

12.3 Nature of Cognition

In the following session, Master Thích Thông Triệt was asked to alter between normal day-to-day discursive thinking (baseline condition) and the practice of "Nature of Cognition[1]" corresponding to the "Bare Cognitive Awareness", the bare cognition of things without reflection and reasoning. The total duration of this run was 12 minutes with 2 min. baseline – 3 min. meditation – 2 min. baseline – 3 min. meditation – 2 min. baseline. With this paradigm one can calculate the difference of the activation levels between the two conditions (t-maps). Regions with a significant increase of the activation level in the meditation condition compared to the baseline condition are shown in red. In contrast to this, regions with significant decrease of the activation level in the meditation condition compared to the baseline condition are shown in green or blue.

In this session we found the highest activation in the triangular part of the left inferior frontal gyrus corresponding to the Brodmann area 46 (BA 46). This region plays a role in sustaining attention and working memory and is involved in exhibiting self-control. The highest deactivation was found in the orbital part of the left middle frontal gyrus which belongs to Brodmann area 10 (BA 10). This region is involved in strategic processes, in memory recall and various executive functions.

---

[1] Also referred to in this book as "Ultimate Cognitive Awareness".

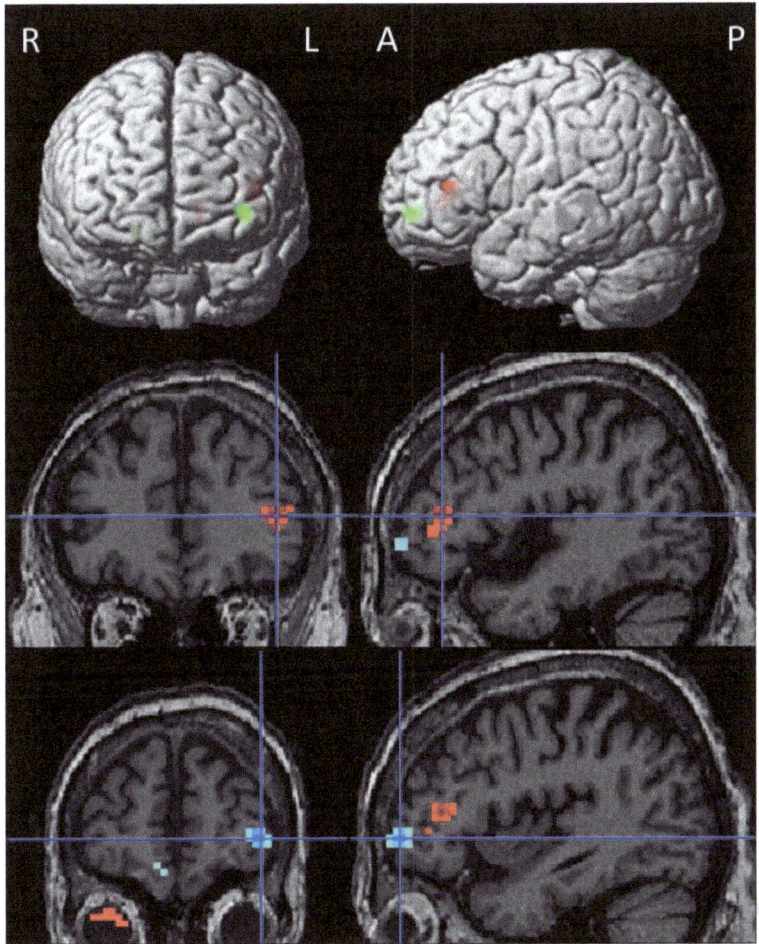

Figure 7: Different activation levels between "Nature of Cognition" and baseline condition (day-to-day thinking). Upper row: Brain surface from front and left; Middle row: coronal and sagittal plane in the triangular part of the left inferior frontal gyrus (BA 46); Lower row: coronal and sagittal plane in the orbital part of the left middle frontal gyrus (BA 10). Increased activation in "Nature of

Cognition" compared to "day-to-day thinking" is shown in red, decreased activation is shown in green or blue.

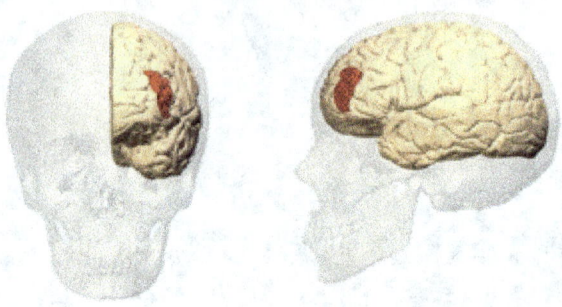

Figure 8: Schematic position of Brodmann Area 46

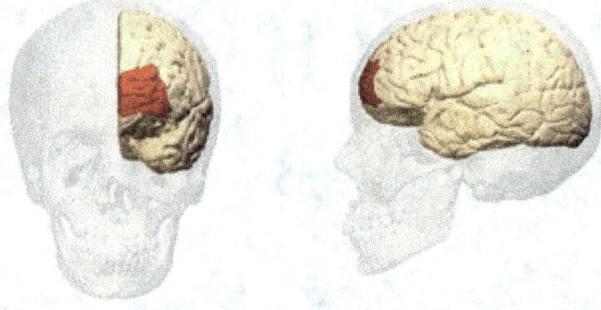

Figure 9: Schematic position of Brodmann Area 10

12.4 Different levels of thinking

In a further session, we used again the block design to distinguish between different levels of thinking. To be more sensitive, we used a block length of 30 seconds and altered between four conditions: "Count", "Intellect", "Mind base"[1], and "Consciousness". The control condition

---

[1] Also referred to in this book as "Thinking Faculty".

"Count" was counting from 1 to 10 with inner speech ("Đếm Thầm số 1 – 10", o). The first activation condition "Intellect" was discursive thinking about objects, interpretation or their relation to other things, and making plans for the future ("Trí Năng", I). The second activation condition "Mind base" was to ruminate, to speculate, and to remember objects and their relation to one self ("Ý Căn", M). The third activation condition "Consciousness" was to differentiate, to compare, and to evaluate objects and their relation to the context and environment ("Ý Thức", C). The four conditions were presented on the display in the order o-I-M-C-o-M-I-C-o-M-C-I-o-C-I-M-o-I-C-M-o. So each condition occurred 5 times in the whole measurement of 10 minutes and 30 seconds.

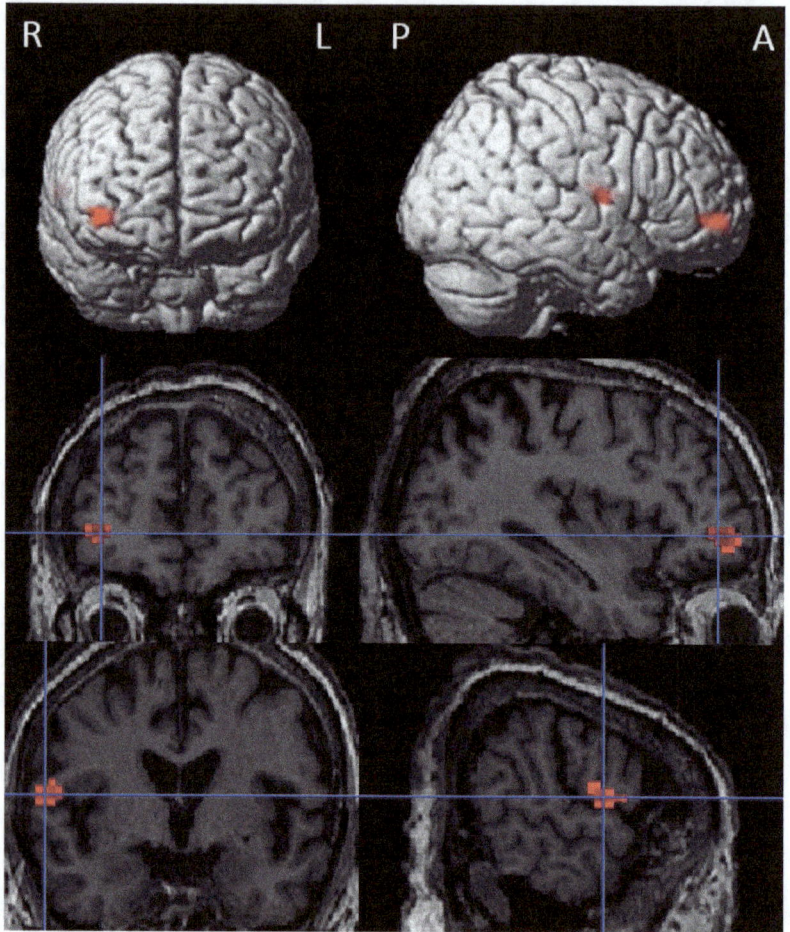

Figure 10: Different activation levels between "Consciousness" and baseline condition ("Count from 1 to 10"). Upper row: Brain surface from front and right; Middle row: coronal and sagittal plane in the orbital part of the right middle frontal gyrus (BA 10); Lower row: coronal and sagittal plane in the right rolandic operculum (BA 43). Increased activation in "Consciousness" compared to "Count" is shown in red, decreased activation is shown in green or blue.

For the condition "Intellect" we found increased activation in the orbital part of the left middle frontal gyrus (BA 10), the same region which was decreased in the "Nature of Cognition" condition described before and which seems to be connected to day-to-day thinking. For the condition "Consciousness" we found increased activation on the other side, in the orbital part of the right middle frontal gyrus (BA 10) and in the right rolandic operculum (BA 43).

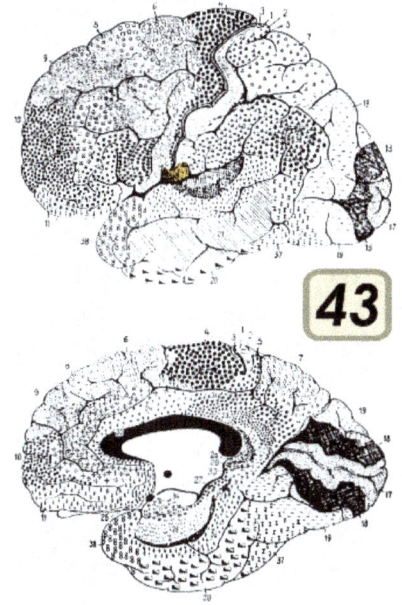

Figure 11: Schematic position of Brodmann Area 43

Conclusion

In the three states of breathing meditation, we found considerable changes in the correlation structure between the four relay stations of the human brain. In the first two states (inner speech and tacit awareness), the correlation between the precuneus and the other relay stations decreased corresponding to the hierarchy level, highest correlation with the thalamus, lower correlation with the hypothalamus, and smallest (or even negative) correlation with the reticular formation. In contrast to this, the third stage (awakening awareness) resulted in equal correlation with all three structures.

Network structure also changed in the "Bare Cognitive Awareness" Meditation session showing higher eigenvector centrality of the left Heschl's gyrus, the primary auditory cortex, and lower eigenvector centrality of the posterior part of the left superior temporal gyrus and the left angular gyrus, structures involved in semantic language processing.

In the meditation session with "Nature of Cognition" altered with day-to-day discursive thinking, we could show a decrease of activity in the left BA 10, which is mainly engaged in verbal reasoning and planning, and an increase in the left BA 46, which is related to attention and self-control.

The investigation of the different levels of thinking showed a shift of activation in the middle frontal gyrus (BA 10) from the left side (as in the day-to-day thinking condition) to the corresponding structure on the right side engaged in context processing.

Acknowledgements

We thank all supporters from Śūnyatā Meditation Association who helped to realize these measurements.

Special thanks to Ashish Kaul Sahib and Bankim Chander for assistance with applying the 256 channel EEG system and performing the measurements. We also thank Prof. Dr.

Klaus Scheffler from the Department of Biomedical Magnetic Resonance, Tübingen University Hospital, Germany for providing the opportunity to use time and the equipment to perform this study.

References

Lohmann G, Margulies DS, Horstmann A, Pleger B, Lepsien J, Goldhahn D, Schloegl H, Stumvoll M, Villringer A, Turner R.: Eigenvector centrality mapping for analyzing connectivity patterns in fMRI data of the human brain. PLoS One. 2010 Apr 27;5(4):e10232. doi: 10.1371/journal.pone.0010232.

The schematic pictures of the brain regions were taken from http://en.wikipedia.org/wiki/ and http://gehirnlernen.de

About the author of this article

Michael Erb (michael.erb@med.uni-tuebingen.de) studied physics at the Universities of Karlsruhe and Tübingen, Germany, and graduated in 1985. He pursued his Ph.D. Studies on artificial neural networks at the Max Planck Institute for Biological Cybernetic in Tübingen from 1986–1990. After a research visit at the Institute for Brain Research, University of Düsseldorf, he became a research fellow at the Institute for Neurophysics, University of Marburg, Germany.

From 1995-2011, he has been a research fellow at the Department of Neuroradiology, University of Tübingen, performing fMRI studies on several topics. Since 2011, he has been a research fellow at the Department of Biomedical Magnetic Resonance, University of Tübingen and since 2012 guest scientist at the Max Planck Institute for Biological Cybernetic in Tübingen. He is involved in building MR compatible stimulation devices and programming MR pulse sequences and analysis software.

COMMENTARY TREATISE 9:

A DREAM BECAME REALITY

Ms. Minh Tuyền's Address at the Paris' Launch of Master's Book in June 2008

Homage to our Master Sakkamuni Buddha,

Honored venerable Bhikkhus and Bhikkhunis,

Honored guests,

Dear friends and fellow meditation students in Paris,

Ms. Minh Tuyền

Causal conditions gathered for Master

Causal conditions are a topic often mentioned in Buddhism. We know that causal conditions form a vast and elaborate network: a seed leads to a fruit, which in turn becomes a seed for other fruits. When causal conditions are all present, then an event will certainly take place.

In 2007, causal conditions were completely present, and therefore Master's brain imaging project in Germany became a reality. With its successful completion, a new horizon for Eastern Zen opened in the West.

A DREAM BECAME REALITY

Today, I would like to tell the story of what causal conditions, or more accurately, what network of causal conditions, have resulted in the brain imaging project involving Master and members of the Sunyata Sangha. In fact, the story that I am recounting today covers only those causal conditions in which I had the opportunity to play a part by having an *intent* and making effort to create causal conditions in favor of the brain imaging project.

Let us go back to the year 2002.

In 2002, Master came to Germany to conduct his second Fundamental Meditation class, together with public lectures on Saturday and Sunday. On Saturday, my husband Quang Trí went to the lecture and asked me to come with him. I declined, offering as excuse that I had to stay home with our child. At the time, I did not have a need to know more about Buddhism. In truth, I dreaded going to lectures on Buddhism as I often could not understand the sermons expounded by the venerable Buddhist monks.

That night, after attending the lecture, Quang Trí came home, recounted the lecture to me, and advised me to attend the following day's lecture. Quang Trí told me that this Buddhist monk was a very good teacher; he used simple, easy to understand terms, and unlike many other Buddhist monks, he provided practical exercises that are easy to do and accord with the scientific method. Quang Trí told me that I would enjoy the lecture. I listened to Quang Trí in a non-committal way.

The following morning, on Sunday, Quang Trí continued to beg, urge and convince me to go. He absolutely wanted me to attend the lecture. I agreed, just to please him. I intended to attend the lecture *just to let the matter rest*. To my surprise, when I met Master and heard his lecture, I found that his teaching and practice method were excellent, very scientific, and very appropriate to the level of understanding of people attending the session. I subsequently registered to attend the meditation class and have been studying with Master until this day. It has now been six years.

On reflection, that was a great beneficial result for me to have met the Dhamma and my Master. This result was caused by Master's presence in Germany; another equally important cause was the stubbornness of Quang Trí! As I reflect on this episode, I can see that this result that was beneficial to me personally had become a beneficial cause as it provided me the opportunity to help Master in the brain imaging project in 2007.

In 2004, the Stuttgart Sunyata Practice Community organized its first Fundamental Meditation class for German speaking people. As my daughter and niece attended this class, I also attended to help with the translation work.

One day, during a break, I heard Master, a few German attendees, and Mr. Quang Chiếu discuss a brain imaging project. Master intended to seek the help of a German attendee who was a senior engineer at Siemens to put him in contact with Siemens and progress the matter, as Siemens was a manufacturer of MRI machines.

He subsequently let Master know that he was not able to progress the matter further.

I had read at the time a magazine article about a brain research using MRI machine conducted by a scientist named Otto Giessen. When I heard Master's intention, I informed Master of this article and offered to liaise with

Mr. Otto Giessen to try progress the brain imaging project. I remembered that Master said to me then: "I entrust this project to Quang Trí and you". Master also said that he could pay 2,000 Euros toward Mr. Otto taking images of his brain.

When I contacted Mr. Otto, he declined and informed me that he could not perform brain imaging for a single individual person. I was surprised and could not understand why it was not possible to perform brain imaging for a single individual person.

I then sought the help of the husband of a friend who was a university professor. He also let me know that this was not possible as it was very difficult to perform brain imaging for just one person. I really could not understand why it was so difficult to arrange MRI imaging. I thought that taking images of the brain should be a simple matter, and could not understand why everyone found it so difficult. Furthermore, 2,000 Euros was not a small amount of money, why didn't they accept to do the work?

It was only later that I understood that f-MRI was a new technology, and at the time there was no *normal baseline* data that could be used to compare images of areas of the cerebral cortex or inside the brain. In the case of blood pressure, for example, scientists need to take the blood pressure of hundreds of people to determine that the normal baseline pressure is about 90 to 120. This has resulted in readings above 120 to be classified as high blood pressure. In the case of MRI imaging, scientists did not have baseline data on the location of areas of the brain. If scientists wanted to determine the location of brain areas, they would need to establish first the baseline data by taking brain images of many people, and not of a single individual.

The second issue was that the MRI machine yields an enormous amount of data. Taking brain images for a single person may only take one or two hours, but scientists will need to follow up by several days of analysis in order to come up with a few diagnoses. The sum of 2,000 Euros was not sufficient to pay for these efforts, and this was the reason why *I was met with refusal each time I knocked on a door.*

I must add that, at the time, Quang Trí was helping me by contacting hospitals where he worked, but was met with the same difficulties as mentioned above.

At the end of 2005, I went to work at the University of Tübingen. There, I met a friend, Ms. Bacher. I mentioned to her the difficulties that I encountered in trying to arrange brain imaging for Master. She offered to contact a friend who was a doctor working in a private practice to see whether he would undertake the work. He answered that this was very difficult and could not be done, but was kind enough to refer me to the Department of Radioneurology at the University of Medicine in Tübingen, South Germany.

I subsequently contacted the department and presented Master's wish to take images of the four ultimate faculties in order to prove the teaching of the Buddha. They agreed.

The preparatory work took over half a year. In 2006, Dr. Michael Erb proposed to start with a trial by taking brain images of two meditation students in order to determine the location in the brain of the four ultimate faculties: Ultimate Seeing, Ultimate Hearing, Ultimate Touch, and Ultimate Cognitive Awareness, as well as areas associated with thinking, inner talk (vitakka), and inner dialogue (vicāra). The Stuttgart Sunyata Practice Community nominated Ms.

A DREAM BECAME REALITY

Minh Vân and Mr. Quang Nguyên for this trial brain imaging.

In June 2007, when Master arrived in Germany to conduct meditation classes, the program to take brain images of Master and members of the Sunyata Sangha really commenced. To this date, in 2008, the program is progressing well. A tangible outcome was that Master was able to prove the existence of the four ultimate faculties that the Buddha mentioned in the Bāhiya sutta.

If we look back carefully, we can see a chain of favorable causal conditions that have combined to bring this outcome: that Master was able to prove that Buddhist Zen is an experimental spiritual science. And who knows if this result may lead to further favorable outcomes: would the 21st century become the time when *scientific Buddhism* appears in the Western hemisphere?

I would like to finish here, thank you for your attention.

Homage to our Master Sakkamuni Buddha.

Brain Imaging Program in Stuttgart

Causal conditions

In the first Fundamental Meditation class conducted in Germany over three days, from June 2nd to June 4th, 2005, at AWO Böblingen, there were 12 German participants. Among them were a couple from Erlangen, Mr. and Mrs. Vogtmeyer. Mr. Vogtmeyer worked at Siemens and his father was a professor at the Technology University at Munchen where he had many Vietnamese students. The ensuing good relationships led Mr. Vogtmeyer to enroll into the meditation class which was conducted by Master Thích Thông Triệt. During this class, he was very interested when he saw Master use an EEG (electroencephalogram) machine to measure the students' brain waves when they entered samādhi. He expressed the opinion that Master should undertake a brain imaging program to demonstrate the brain location of the ultimate faculties that Master taught about.

He contacted his brother who was a medical doctor and neurologist working in the USA. His brother informed him that there were already too many brain studies in the USA, and therefore this idea, unfortunately, could not be progressed. This was a first causal condition suggesting that a brain imaging program could be performed on Master.

It wasn't until 2006 that this program became a reality with the help of Ms. Minh Tuyền Phạm Ngọc Thịnh and Mr. Quang Trí Phạm Văn Phú and their contact at the University of Tübingen. Ms. Minh Tuyền was previously a dentistry student at the Medical University at Tübingen and still maintained her contacts there. A German friend informed her that she should contact the Department of Neuroradiology on this matter.

Their first contact was with Dr. Michael Erb, a professor at the Department of Neuroradiology, who then contacted Dr. Ranganatha Sitaram from the Institute of Medical Psychology. Together, they conducted the brain imaging program on Master.

In order to bring clarity to the research on the location of the ultimate faculties inside the brain, Master expounded to Dr. Erb and Dr. Sitaram the Bāhiya Sutta where the Buddha mentioned these ultimate faculties more than 2,500 years ago. Ultimate Seeing and Ultimate Hearing were located by scientists in 1992, however Ultimate Touch and Ultimate Cognitive Awareness have not yet been identified.

In the scientific research about the human mind, scientists have long abandoned the search for a location within the brain that controls people's emotions and actions.

Master was the first person who wanted to demonstrate that, by following the teaching of the Buddha, one could control the verbal chatter in the mind which would then activate the three ultimate faculties of the Wordless Awareness Mind.

This was a new idea that had not previously been mentioned in the practice of Zen.

I can feel the compassion of Master in his endeavor to demonstrate to meditation students the validity of his teaching.

I remember a discussion that Dr. Erb had with seven German meditation groups in AWO Böblingen in June 2008. Mrs. Erb told the group that she didn't know much about her husband's research into Master's brain, but she could tell, by observing Master's demeanor, countenance, and aura, that Zen had brought true blissfulness to Master.

A method for taking brain images of the ultimate faculties was designed by the two researchers and tested with two Sunyata Meditation students in Stuttgart, Mr. Quang Nguyên Tô Đình Hải and Ms. Minh Vân Nguyễn Thị Vân, in December 2006.

During an interval of 12 minutes, the students lying inside the MRI machine would, on cue from instructions displayed on a screen, perform two minutes of thinking, followed by three minutes of meditation on one of the ultimate faculty topics of the experiment (*refer to the method for taking images of Ultimate Hearing below*).

The difficulty with this method resides in the ability of the Zen practitioner to switch from a thinking state to a meditative state in a very short period of time while showing a sufficiently large difference between the two states that can be recorded in the experiment.

In the case of Master, the first difficulty that Master encountered during his brain imaging experiments was how to think with intensity during the two minutes of the *thinking* phase. I think that none of Master's students had difficulty with this phase.

The majority of the brain imaging program involving Master was performed while Master travelled to Germany to teach. His teaching commitments were very onerous, and in addition, Master had to spend time at night to prepare further reading materials. This caused unfavorable health issues for Master when he had to spend stretches of three or four hours inside the MRI machine.

It was not until January 2010 that, on the invitation of Dr. Erb, Master travelled to Germany for a week dedicated to the brain imaging experiments. That week was very fruitful. Master suggested for the first time to take images of brain areas that Master had wanted to know about for a very long time.

In addition to imaging the brain areas that correspond to the ultimate faculties as in previous years, Master suggested taking images of the pre-frontal cortex corresponding to the Thinking Faculty, Consciousness and Intellect. He wanted to see their relationship with the Broca and Wernicke areas as well as areas of inner talk and inner dialogue. Dr. Erb didn't expect that Master could activate each of these areas separately in his brain. I was also full of anticipation about the results of these experiments. We also conducted the imaging of other practice methods such as Hearing-things-as-they-are and Seeing-things-as-they-are.

Another innovation that we did was to take images of Master's brain while he went through the four stages of meditation of the Buddha. Results were very clear. Dr. Michael Erb and Dr. Ranganatha Sitaram decided to present the results of this experiment at the Annual Meeting of the OHBM (Organization for Human Brain Mapping) in June 2010 in Barcelona, Spain.

Brain imaging program Phase 1

The following is a summary of the brain imaging program involving Master, members of the Sunyata Sangha, and meditation students from December 2006 to January 2010.

1. On December 15th, 2006, brain imaging of meditation students Quang Nguyên and Minh Vân.

2. From June 5th, 2007 to June 19th, 2007, brain imaging of Master Thích Thông Triệt, Bhikkhu Không Phổ, Bhikkhuni Triệt Như, Bhikkhuni Tường Liên and meditation student Minh Huệ.

3. On May 13th, 2008, brain imaging of Master Thích Thông Triệt and Bhikkhuni Triệt Như.

4. On May 26th, 2009, brain imaging of meditation students Quang Nguyên and Quang Chiếu.

5. On June 11th, 2009, brain imaging of Master Thích Thông Triệt.

6. On December 22nd, 2009, brain imaging of meditation student Quang Chiếu using a new method.

7. On January 16th, 2010 and 17 January 17th, 2010, brain imaging of Master Thích Thông Triệt.

After five years of experimentation, Dr. Michael Erb and Dr. Ranganatha Sitaram represented the University of Tübingen at the Annual Meeting of the Organization on Human Brain Mapping (OHBM) conducted from June 6th to June 11th, 2010 in Barcelona, Spain.

Dr. Michael Erb and Dr. Ranganatha Sitaram displayed and presented the results of brain imaging undertaken on Master and Sunyata meditation students while they went through various meditation practices.

This outcome was a matter of great encouragement for Master and all Sunyata meditation students in Stuttgart who had contributed to the brain imaging program.

Before ending this article on the Stuttgart brain imaging program, we wish to express our sincere gratitude toward

A DREAM BECAME REALITY

Dr. Michael Erb and Dr. Ranganatha Sitaram who have spent an enormous amount of time over the last five years to ensure that this brain imaging program comes to a successful completion. Most of the imaging sessions took place over weekends or public holidays to take advantage of the availability of the fMRI machine, and Dr. Michael Erb and Dr. Ranganatha Sitaram did not mind working on these days.

Although some of the imaging sessions did not meet expectations, they have remained patient and continued to support us through the program. It is our hope that this book will usher in a new understanding on Zen and neuroscience.

We hope that the results of this brain imaging program will help the University of Tübingen gather new information on its research on the human brain and spirituality, and will help meditation students renew their confidence and vigor in the practice of Zen as taught by Master Thích Thông Triệt.

Method for imaging Ultimate Hearing

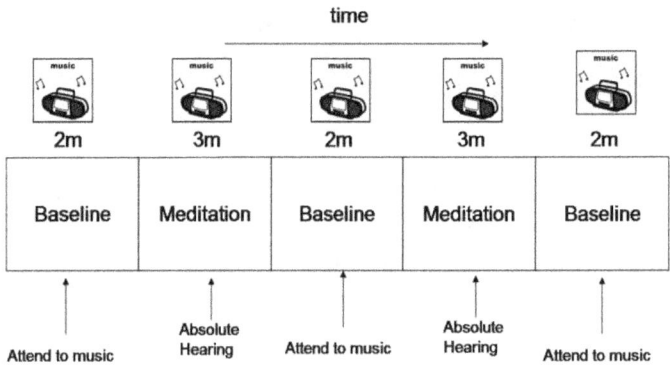

(The instruction Baseline/Meditation can be heard and seen on the small screen inside the fMRI machine)

Brain Imaging Program in 2013

Brain imaging program Phase 2 (2013)

Saturday June 8th, 2013

We started at 9 am and met with the University of Tübingen team of four people led by Dr. Erb. We were informed that a maximum of four participants can be accommodated. Our delegation consisted of Master Thích Thông Triệt, Ms. Thuần Tuệ (who will be the two main people involved in brain imaging), Bhikkhuni Phổ Như, and Mr. Tuệ Sơn who is Master's assistant.

The measurement program consisted of the following:

1. IMAGING OF MASTER'S BRAIN ANATOMY, 5 minutes

This is the first step in every measurement session to determine Master's brain anatomical structure. This step takes 5 minutes.

2. IMAGING OF THE PRECUNEUS and THREE RELAY STATIONS, 42 minutes

Five imaging methods were applied in sequence when taking images of each of the two areas:

- The message "Relax" is displayed on screen. Master stays in a relaxed state for 10 minutes, with little thinking. This is a fundamental step used as baseline for comparison with the other measurement steps.

- The message "Meditation" is displayed on screen. Master practices the breathing method taught by the Buddha (ānapānasati samādhi, awareness-of-breathing-in-and- breathing-out samādhi) continuously for 10 minutes, consisting of three steps:

1. Verbal breathing. – In this step, Master applied the "verbal breathing" method which consists of saying silently "I am aware of breathing in, I am aware of breathing out" while breathing in and out steadily. The Buddha called this state "samādhi with inner talk and inner dialogue". This step lasts 2 minutes.

Note:

When practicing the Awareness-of-breathing-in-and breathing-out method, nerve impulses from the reticular formation located in the pons immediately activated the third relay station which is the hypothalamus. At the same time, nerve impulses from the pons also directly reached the fourth relay station which is the precuneus. When referencing neuroscience, Master considers the precuneus to be the seat of self- cognitive awareness. Master considers the precuneus to be equivalent to the "Tathā-Mind" as referenced in Buddhist meditation, and to "Buddha-nature" as referenced in Zen Buddhism.

2. Non-verbal breathing. – In this step, Master breathed in and out for 4 minutes while maintaining a "silent awareness". If the practitioner truly experiences silent awareness, they would attain the state that the Buddha called "samādhi without inner talk and inner dialogue".

3. Breathing with "awake awareness". In this step, Master applied for 4 minutes the method of breathing with a clear and awake awareness while there is no verbal chatter in the mind.

Note: the three processes of breathing in and out mentioned above were taught by the Buddha and recorded as the sutta on Breathing-In and Breathing-Out Samādhi (ānapānasati samādhi).

When applying the Awareness-of-breathing-in-and-breathing-out Samādhi method, nerve impulses from the first relay station will go straight to the third relay station (the hypothalamus). At the same time, nerve impulses are also sent from the pons directly to the fourth relay station, which is the precuneus.

- The message "Cognitive Awareness" is displayed on screen. Master continued to apply the breathing method as taught by the Buddha. Then, while evoking the Bare Cognition topic, Master continued breathing for another 10 minutes to enter deeper states of samādhi. Finally the state of automatic breathing ("pure breathing") appeared, indicating the state of samādhi that the Buddha called "immobility samādhi".

- The words "Baseline" and "Meditation" are displayed on screen. Master activated his Ultimate Cognitive Awareness faculty through a sequence of 2 minutes thinking, 3 minutes meditation, 2 minutes thinking, 3 minutes meditation, 2 minutes thinking for a total of 12 minutes. He kept all three mental formation processes silent. The hypothalamus and the language areas, consisting of the Broca, Wernicke, inner talk, and inner dialogue areas, appeared as green while the precuneus on the left hemisphere appeared as red.

- The words "Baseline" and "Meditation" are displayed on screen. Master activated the three ultimate faculties in turn: Ultimate Seeing, Ultimate Hearing, and Ultimate Touch. For each ultimate faculty, the sequence consists of 2 minutes thinking, 3 minutes meditation, 2 minutes thinking, 3 minutes meditation, 2 minutes thinking for a total of 12 minutes.

1. Activating Ultimate Seeing: by looking at an object while not naming the object in the mind. The cuneus area in the occipital lobe immediately appeared as red.

2. Activating Ultimate Hearing: by hearing a sound but not repeating the content of the sound in the mind. The Ultimate Hearing area in the temporal lobe immediately appeared as red. Interestingly, the cerebellum also appeared as green.

3. Activating Ultimate Touch by applying the Just Knowing technique, or being aware of an object but not naming it, or Bare Attention technique. Through breathing, or brushing the hand, or relaxing the tongue for 5 minutes, the Ultimate Touch area in the parietal lobe appeared as red.

We had confirmation that the reticular formation, thalamus, hypothalamus, and precuneus are activated synchronously if they have the same level of intensity. However, the results did not confirm whether the sequence of activation of the four relay stations goes from the first relay station to the fourth relay station as Master predicted. This point can only be validated by further imaging of Master's brain using the DTI method.

3. IMAGING OF THE THREE CINGULATE GYRUS AREAS, 30 minutes

A. Anterior cingulate gyrus

Imaging of the anterior cingulate gyrus was performed by applying the technique of immobility of speech mental formation.

Master performed seeing and hearing with thinking and pressed a button to indicate that he had performed the task. The step takes 10 minutes with an optimal interval between button presses of 20 seconds.

When Master performed seeing and hearing with thinking, the anterior cingulate gyrus appeared as red. When Master performed seeing and hearing without thinking, the anterior cingulate gyrus appeared as green.

B. Mid cingulate gyrus

Imaging of the mid cingulate gyrus was performed by applying the technique of immobility of the Feelings and Sensations aggregate and Perception aggregate.

Master performed breathing for 10 minutes while external touch was applied by brushing his hand.

When Master experienced touch while Feelings and Sensations and Perception are activated, the mid cingulate gyrus appeared as red.

When Master experienced touch while Feelings and Sensations and Perception are immobile, the mid cingulate gyrus appeared as green.

C. Posterior cingulate gyrus

Imaging of the posterior cingulate gyrus was performed by applying the technique of immobility of thought mental formation.

Master performed seeing and hearing for 10 minutes without any verbal chatter in the mind. The posterior cingulate gyrus appeared as green.

4. BRAIN IMAGING USING THE DTI METHOD, 20 minutes

This step was performed over 20 minutes.

5. IMAGING OF THE INNER TALK AND INNER DIALOGUE AREAS, 10 minutes and 30 seconds

Imaging of the Thinking Faculty, Consciousness and Intellect areas.

Each block starts with a message displayed on screen.

A. Silently counting for 30 seconds.

B. Activating the Intellect for 30 seconds (seeing an image or hearing a sound, and making inferences).

C. Activating the Thinking Faculty for 30 seconds (seeing an image or hearing a sound, and remembering and thinking).

D. Activating the Consciousness for 30 seconds (if seeing an image or hearing a sound while having no thought of comparison and differentiating, this area is absent).

The step consists of five iterations for a total duration of 10 minutes and 30 seconds.

6. INNER TALK, INNER DIALOGUE AND BROCA AREAS, 8 minutes

Each block starts with a message displayed on screen.

A. Silently counting for 30 seconds.

C. Performing inner talk for 30 seconds.

C. Performing silent inner dialogue for 30 seconds.

The step consists of five iterations for a total duration of 8 minutes.

7. **IMAGING THE SYMPATHETIC AND PARASYMPATHETIC NERVOUS SYSTEMS, 10 minutes**

Messages are displayed on screen with the words "Yoga meditation" and "Buddhist meditation".

When Master performed the Yoga breathing method (with concentration, focusing attention or following), the sympathetic nervous system was activated.

When Master performed the Buddhist breathing method, the parasympathetic nervous system was activated.

Master performed Yoga breathing and Buddhist breathing methods alternatively for 30 seconds, totaling 2 iterations of 5 minutes each.

8. **IDENTIFYING IMAGES AND SOUNDS DISPLAYED ON SCREEN, 6 minutes, and completion of measurement program.**

Sindelfingen, March 18th, 2013
Quang Chiếu

A New Horizon

Foundations of a spiritual science

Zen is an experimental spiritual science. First comes an *awakening*, then a *practice*, and finally the *results* of experiencing what we have awakened to (realized) and practiced. These three processes are always intimately linked. Awakening is based on hearing and thinking. Experiencing is based on practice. Only through practice can we have an inner experience on the three levels of body, mind, and spiritual wisdom of what we have been awakened to. Spiritual wisdom belongs in the innovative mind and is the basis of innovative ways. When the practitioner reaches this point, they have the ability to demonstrate what they say or teach with experimental data, albeit within a narrow area of focus. This is the fundamental model of an experimental spiritual science.

Reconciling with the Three Forms of Wisdom

The Buddhist Three Forms of Wisdom – Listen, Reflect, and Practice – are three components that cannot be split apart in Buddhist meditation. At all three levels of study, Fundamental, Intermediate, and Advanced, the practitioner needs to apply the model of the Three Forms of Wisdom (Listen, Reflect, Practice) in order to demonstrate the strong interaction between the teaching and the practice through their own practical experience. One cannot have an awakening and not practice, and one cannot practice without realizing (or being awakened to) the principles underlying one's method of practice.

Value of teaching and practice method

The teaching is the theory while the practice method teaches us how to practice. Theory and practice cannot be separated. The practice demonstrates the value of the theory through the inner experience of the practitioner on their body, mind, and spiritual wisdom. Thoroughly knowing the theory but without practicing is the way of scholars who study and remember well suttas and commentaries without knowing how to get started on the path that leads to the ultimate enlightenment. On the other hand, practice without theory is like fighting without any method and *hitting things at random*, which will ultimately lead to damage to body and mind, going from no illness to illness, and from little illness to serious illness. Examples of such illnesses are disturbances to the cardiovascular system, internal organs, or nervous system.

The suttas and commentaries often mention the Three Forms of Wisdom (consisting of Listening, Reflecting, and Practicing) as the fundamental spiritual principles, in which practice plays a deciding role in achieving success. Practice is the process of experiencing what we have listened to and reflected on. Eventually, through the various stages of practice or training, we achieve the ultimate result which is experiencing the theory that we have cognized. Through this result we will be able to demonstrate what we have learnt as theory. For this reason, Zen is an experimental spiritual science. It is built upon the dual foundations of theory and practice. Theory is the basis for experiencing. Practice is the factual demonstration of the validity of the theory. Those who are enamored with the theory and forgo practice are savants, busybodies, and chatterboxes. They love to talk but what they say is empty, like the saying "empty vessels make most noise". These savants and chatterboxes become speechless if they are suddenly asked how to practice in order to arrive at the ultimate destination. On the other hand, those who only like to practice without relying on theory are over-enthusiastic people who lack the wisdom to judge or ascertain what eventual benefits this practice will bring to their body, mind, and spiritual wisdom.

A dream became reality

Twenty years ago, I pondered much upon what happens in the cerebral cortex and inside the brain when a person is experiencing samādhi. I hypothesized that when we enter samādhi, all the areas of the brain that are involved in false thoughts such as memory areas, thinking areas, the Intellect, Broca area, inner talk area, hypothalamus and Wernicke are immediately "shut". At the same time, the cognitive awareness area became "active". This was the reasoning that I adopted.

It wasn't until June 2007 that these hypotheses were validated with the brain imaging experiments using the fMRI equipment. They became reality. On the afternoon of June 14th, before closing the Buddhist Psychology class, I joyfully told the class:

- With the images recorded by the fMRI equipment, I have fulfilled my wishes. First, I have finally proven that the cognitive awareness area and the touch area are both located at the rear of the left hemisphere of the brain just as I have taught you for a long time! Second, we have demonstrated that when we enter the state of samādhi, the pre-frontal cortex areas and the two language areas which are the Broca and Wernicke areas are all silent. Third, we have demonstrated the existence of a chain reaction between the cognitive awareness area and the limbic system located inside the brain. Fourth, we have demonstrated that when we enter samādhi, the brain wave goes into the delta range, heart rate slows, and breathing becomes very slow, and occasionally falls into the pattern of automatic breathing ("pure breathing"). There is one point that still needs to be proven: what is the form of the magnetic energy field generated by the cognitive awareness area? This point will need a further set of favorable causal conditions in order to be elucidated.

Praising the merits

I said to meditation students Phú and Thịnh:

" – Today's accomplishment marks an important step forward in my dhamma teaching journey. You have both contributed greatly in helping me demonstrate the validity of Buddhist Zen in the light of 21st century scientific knowledge.

My dream of being able to demonstrate the location of the areas that I have described in my classes around the world has finally become a reality. I am most satisfied that the cognitive awareness and touch areas have been demonstrated to be located where I thought them to be. From today, a new horizon for Zen has become wide open! Through this scientific experiment, we have now been able to demonstrate the existence of the four Ultimate Faculties that the Buddha taught to Bāhiya as recorded in the Minor Discourses of the Buddha (Khuddaka Nikāya), Enlightenment Chapter (Bodhi Vagga).

Seventeen years ago, in November 1997, during the third Fundamental Meditation course that was organized in Corona, Southern California, by Bhikkhuni Triệt Như, who was at the time a lay Buddhist under the name of Từ Tâm

Thảo, I used an electroencephalogram (EEG) machine to measure students' brain waves when they practiced the practical exercises and meditation techniques that I taught. This was, at the time, a substantial advance in the practice of Zen in the USA which was worthy of encouragement.

Then in 2007, you helped me concretized the second step forward which was to demonstrate, using the fMRI brain imaging equipment, the working of the brain when we enter the state of samādhi! Once again, I praise your spirit of service to Buddhism."

BUILDING ON A DREAM

I wish to take this opportunity to briefly describe the process by which my dream of taking images of the brain has become a reality.

Thoughts of experimentation

During my time in Seattle, Washington State (1992-1994) and at Beaverton, Oregon (1994-1997), I had the opportunity to visit two large libraries located in the schools of medicine of these two cities. It was then that my knowledge of the brain, the nervous system, the immune system, psychology, functions of the blood, and biochemical substances secreted by endocrine glands was built and systematized from the old knowledge that I had pre-1975. Every day, I spent time studying in the libraries and reconciled what I learnt with what I experienced when I practiced my practical exercises and meditation techniques.

What excited me the most was my "discovery" of materials about the brain, mind, body, nervous system, and biochemical substances inside the human body. I had a very clear answer to the question that had been on my mind since 1982: when we practice Zen correctly, our body becomes healthy through the biochemical acetylcholine; when we practice Zen incorrectly, our body becomes ill due to the biochemicals norepinephrine and epinephrine.

At the beginning of 1993, I read an article in the Scientific American magazine about the location of the seeing and hearing areas in the rear left hemisphere. I subsequently searched for articles that talked about this "rear left hemisphere" area.

At the time I began to form the thought that one day I would be able to take images of my brain to determine how the pre-frontal cortex areas, the triangular area forming the Wordless Awareness Mind, and areas deep inside the brain would appear when I enter the state of samādhi. In essence, I wished to get help from science to obtain tangible proof of the Ultimate Cognitive Awareness faculty that the Buddha referred to 2,500 years ago.

I often say: "The East can explain and execute, but is unable to point to scientific evidence. On the other hand, the West can explain and point to scientific evidence but does not know how to execute." I now wanted to get help from science to successfully point to what I wanted to point to. Where is the actual location in the cerebral cortex of the cognitive awareness and touch areas? What is the interaction between the cognitive awareness structures and the limbic system? How does the concept of "the three ultimate faculties are simultaneously open" appear in the triangular area at the junction of the occipital, temporal and parietal lobes in the rear left hemisphere when we practice techniques such as bare attention, or walking meditation with no verbal chatter?

The meaning of experience

The thought of teaching Buddhist Zen as an experimental spiritual science kept arising in my head. I considered the Buddhist model of "Listen, Reflect, Practice" as the basis of an experimental spiritual science. A spiritual practitioner must go through three processes of experiencing:

1. Listen and Reflect help the practitioner awaken and realize.

2. Practice helps the practitioner internalize.

3. Only through internalization can the practitioner have an inner experience involving the three aspects of body, mind, and spiritual development. This is the meaning and value of experiencing. The key to experiencing is the practice. Practice is a way of doing, which must be based on technique and regularity or assiduity. One cannot practice when one feels like it, or practice on some days and not on others.

A person who has a spiritual realization but does not practice has realized a truth but is not able to internalize this truth. A person who practices but who lacks assiduity and appropriate techniques will not be able to experience the truth through the three aspects of body, mind, and spiritual wisdom. It is only through inner experience that the value of experiencing can be established.

The full meaning of experiencing requires both theory and practice.

Using science as a means of reconciliation

In 1996-1997 I published the book "Explaining Zen using Diagrams". My main intent was to explain the teaching of my Master Thích Thanh Từ contained in his book "Vietnamese Zen Buddhism at the End of the Twentieth Century". However, through this book, I also started to introduce neuroscience, the limbic system, endocrine system, meditation techniques, and electroencephalograms into the teaching of Zen.

Subsequently, from 1997 to 2007, all Sunyata Meditation practice communities used electroencephalograms as supporting causal conditions for their practice of samādhi (stillness of mind) meditation and paññā (wisdom) meditation.

Conceptualize first, then demonstrate

Since I started teaching Fundamental Meditation classes and Wisdom Intermediate Level classes to practice communities in the USA, Germany, France, Switzerland, Canada, and Australia, I always said that the touch area is located in the parietal lobe while the cognitive awareness area is located in the middle of the triangle formed by Ultimate Seeing, Ultimate Hearing, and Ultimate Touch. But in reality I had no means of demonstrating the actual location of the touch and cognitive awareness areas.

I remember that during the 41st Fundamental Meditation class held in April 2007 in Northern California, a student who was also a medical doctor kept asking me how I can prove that the cognitive awareness area is located in the rear left hemisphere of the brain. I promised that I would give him proof in August 2008, after I had gone to Germany to teach and perform brain imaging experiments with a university there.

When causal conditions eventually gathered in June 2008, I was able to fulfill the dream that I had 15 years before. It was with the help of the two meditation students Phạm Văn Phú (Quang Trí) and Phạm Ngọc Thịnh (Minh Tuyền) that I could realize this inconceivable dream. My theoretical reasoning was now congruent with scientific experimentation.

Causal conditions began

When I conducted a Fundamental Meditation class to German speaking students organized by the Stuttgart Sunyata Meditation practice community in May 2004, there were four students who took turns to do the translation from Vietnamese into German: (1) Ms. Minh Huệ, (2) Ms. Minh Giác, (3) Ms. Thịnh, and (4) Mr. Phú.

During the class, I used electroencephalograms to show the brain waves that appear when we practice stopping all verbal chatter during samādhi. Our German students were very excited. One of them spoke of a desire to help me realize a brain imaging program that would demonstrate the location in the cerebral cortex of the ultimate faculties of the Wordless Awareness Mind. However, this initiative couldn't be realized as the costs were prohibitive.

In May 2005, I asked Ms. Thịnh and Mr. Phú whether they could find a place that would be able to conduct brain imaging for a cost of 2,000 Euros.

Mr. Phú contacted Professor Otto Ulrith who was in charge of the MRI imaging program at the University of Ciessen in Hanover and asked whether he would consider taking images of my brain. However, causal conditions were still not sufficient as the university could not perform brain imaging on a single individual.

Intention to create causal conditions

Ms. Thịnh became concerned when she saw the failure of the initiative. One day toward the end of 2005, she confided to a colleague who worked as secretary at the Medical and Dentistry School at the University of Tübingen about her difficulty in organizing a brain imaging program for me. Her colleague told her immediately that the University of Tübingen had a Department of Neuroradiology, specializing in taking brain images. She promised to help put Ms. Thịnh in contact with Dr. Michael Erb in order to progress a brain imaging program for me. It was through this introduction to Dr. Michael Erb that Ms. Thịnh realized her wish to help me achieve the dream that I had first had 20 years before.

Causal conditions fully gathered

In the first months of 2006, through several meetings with Dr. Michael Erb, Ms. Thịnh presented him with two practical matters: (1) Her Master is a meditation teacher. He is seeking the help of the Department to take images of the four ultimate sensory faculties: Ultimate Seeing, Ultimate Hearing, Ultimate Touch, and Ultimate Cognitive Awareness to ascertain their location in the cerebral cortex. Master presently only knows about the location of Ultimate Seeing and Ultimate Hearing and not the other two faculties. He is especially eager to know the location of Ultimate Cognitive Awareness in the cerebral cortex. (2) The amount of money that her Master can put toward the brain imaging program is 2,000 Euros.

Dr. Michael Erb just smiled instead of giving an answer to the matter of the 2,000 Euros. He then suggested that Dr. Ranganatha Sitaram talk directly to Ms. Thịnh.

A DREAM BECAME REALITY

On November 9th, 2006, Dr. Sitaram presented Ms. Thịnh with a standard questionnaire consisting of 19 questions in English and asked her to give them to her Master for him to complete. The aim of the questionnaire was to inform Dr. Sitaram of the approach and method of Sunyata meditation, and whether they are similar to other contemporary schools of meditation.

Two days later, on November 13th, Ms. Thịnh emailed the questionnaire to Bhikkhuni Triệt Như. It consisted of the following questions:

Question 1: In what category would you put your meditation practice? Examples are: Vipassanā, Zen, Tibetan traditions, transcendental meditation, Raja Yoga or other forms of Yoga, or Qi Gong, etc.

Question 2: How long have you been following this practice (in months, years)?

Question 3: On average, how many times do you meditate per week?

Question 4: What is the duration of your sitting meditation sessions (30 minutes, one hour)?

Question 5: What is the level of your meditation practice: beginner, intermediate, advanced or any other levels?

Question 6: Do you meditate with eyes open or closed?

Question 7: Does your practice require specific postures or sets of exercises?

Question 8: Do you recite mantras or suttas as part of your practice?

Question 9: Do you use a breathing technique?

Question 10: Do you focus the mind on various parts of the body using your imagination or any other techniques?

Question 11: Does your meditation technique rely on focusing on the object or use any form of contemplation?

Question 12: Should meditation expect any sensations occurring on the body or events occurring in the mind, either constantly or intermittently?

Question 13: If your meditation relies on an object:

- Are there one or several objects of meditation?
- Are these objects mobile or still?
- Do these objects involve looking at external things or hearing sounds? Please describe the objects that you use.

Question 14: If you do not have objects, do you turn your attention to any other things when you meditate? Please describe these things.

Question 15: When you meditate, do you bring into your consciousness any imagining and focusing on something, either constantly or intermittently?

Question 16: When you meditate, do you expect emotions to occur during the session, either constantly or intermittently?

Question 17: If you practice regularly, do you expect a change in perspective?

Question 18: Do you expect changes in behaviors as a result of your meditation?

Question 19: When you practice meditation, do you hope to achieve a transformation of your emotions?

I completed the questionnaire and sent it back to Dr. Sitaram through Ms. Thịnh.

(From left to right) Standing: Quang Chiếu, Minh Tuyền, Bhikkhuni Triệt Như, Dr. Ranganatha Sitaram, Bhikkhu Không Như. Sitting: Master Thích Thông Triệt and Dr. Michael Erb

Trial imaging

Once he knew about the approach of Sunyata meditation and my specific aim of identifying the location of the four ultimate sensory faculties, Dr. Michael Erb immediately accepted our request.

Dr. Erb then suggested to Ms. Thịnh to select two meditation students on whom he can trial the method of imaging Ultimate Seeing, Ultimate Hearing, Ultimate Touch, and Ultimate Cognitive Awareness. As this was the first time that he would be taking brain images under the

Sunyata meditation method, the trial would allow him to be more efficient when he came to taking my brain's images in June 2007. He was also excited by his new discovery of Sunyata meditation through his contacts with Sunyata meditation students, myself and members of the Sunyata sangha.

Volunteers

In August 2006, at a meeting of the Sunyata Stuttgart Practice Community, Ms. Thịnh presented the brain imaging project that she had arranged with the Department of Neuroradiology at the University of Tübingen. The department required two volunteer meditation students from the practice community to come to the university and have their brain images taken. Mr. Quang Nguyên and Ms. Minh Vân volunteered for this exercise.

Request to take brain images of all meditation students at the practice community

As the brain images obtained from Ms. Minh Vân and Mr. Quang Nguyên were quite different from those that he took from other people previously, Dr. Michael Erb offered to Ms. Minh Tuyền to take brain images, free of charge, for all students in the practice community to verify the consistency of the meditation method. He indicated that the first two students showed similar results both when they were in meditation and out of meditation. When they were out of meditation, their pre-frontal cortex showed a high level of activity. When they were in meditation, this area was silent.

Dr. Erb explained in passing to Ms. Minh Tuyền that any person who wished to have their brain images taken would have to pay the university 2,000 Euros for a 15-minute session!

Smooth progress

In May 2007, members of the Sunyata sangha and I went to Germany to conduct two meditation classes (1) the Wisdom Intermediate Level 2 class, and (2) the Advanced Level Buddhist Psychology class.

On June 1st, the brain imaging program for members of the sangha commenced. Over several days afterwards, members of the sangha took turns to have their brain image taken. On June 17th, this series of brain imaging was completed. Everything went smoothly.

As everything was progressing smoothly, Ms. Minh Huệ asked to have her brain image taken on June 19th. Dr. Erb agreed.

Marvelous causal condition

On the morning of June 19th, Ms. Minh Huệ prepared to go and have her brain image taken. I was very tired as I had stayed up until 3 o'clock in the morning writing my book on the Process of Spiritual Cultivation and Realization of the Buddha, but decided to accompany Ms. Minh Huệ to give her moral support.

Quite unexpectedly, Dr. Michael Erb was very glad when he saw me and invited me to have my brain images taken first, before Ms. Minh Huệ. He indicated that he needed to retake images of the cognitive awareness, touch, hearing and seeing areas of my brain. He needed to spend three minutes on each in order to write his summary.

Referring to my belief in the law of causal conditions, I thought that this was a beneficial and marvelous causal condition that would help me complete the brain imaging program. I felt that the outcome of this brain imaging would open a new horizon for my Zen teaching method in keeping with this 21st century space age.

Where is the touch area?

Dr. Sitaram explained the protocol for this round of experimentation: 3 minutes of meditation using Ultimate Seeing, then 3 minutes using Ultimate Cognitive Awareness, then 3 minutes using Ultimate Hearing, then 3 minutes using Ultimate Cognitive Awareness and finally 3 minutes using Ultimate Touch and 3 minutes using Ultimate Cognitive Awareness. The focus of this last round of imaging is the touch and cognitive awareness areas.

I remembered that over the last few days, I was unsure of the exact location of the touch area in the cerebral cortex of the rear left hemisphere. I would apply in this occasion the technique of Bare Attention in seeing, hearing and touch meditations and see the location of these three ultimate faculties in the cerebral cortex of the rear left hemisphere.

After spending over an hour in the machine practicing under external instructions and successively activating the four ultimate faculties of Ultimate Seeing, Ultimate Hearing, Ultimate Touch and Ultimate Cognitive Awareness, I heard Ms. Minh Huệ notifying me: "It's completed". This was followed by my answering a questionnaire in German which Ms. Minh Huệ translated for me, while I was still lying inside the machine.

Outside the machine, Dr. Sitaram and Dr. Erb were following on screen the activities of the various cerebral cortex areas of my brain.

Dr. Erb let me know that that day's session yielded clear images of various areas of the cerebral cortex, from the

A DREAM BECAME REALITY

frontal lobe to the three areas in the rear left hemisphere. Dr. Sitaram also let me know that he would give the day's results to Ms. Thịnh. About two weeks later, I received in America the preliminary summary of results showing activities of areas of the cerebral cortex, inner parts of the brain, cardiovascular system, and breathing while I was in meditation and out of meditation.

After me, it was Ms. Minh Huệ's turn to have her brain image taken. The following day, on June 20th, members of the Sunyata sangha and I flew back to the USA.

A joy for all

Question: Master, in what year did these events occur?

Answer: It was in 2007, the first year in which members of the Sunyata sangha and I had our brain images taken. Following that, in 2008, 2009, 2010 and at the end of 2013, I went to Germany to conduct classes and again had my brain images taken. Results became clearer and clearer as we progressed.

Question: Master, could you tell us your impressions of the brain imaging program over the last few years?

Answer: From 1993, I have always dreamt of taking images of the brain while in the state of samādhi in order to provide scientific evidence for the Buddha's teaching. Now, in 2014, this brain imaging program has been completed. I have been able to provide evidence of:

- The location of the four ultimate faculties: Ultimate Seeing, Ultimate Hearing, Ultimate Touch and Ultimate Cognitive Awareness. These four ultimate faculties are all present when I enter the state of samādhi.

- The precuneus area is active when one is in a state of deep samādhi.

- At the same time, areas associated with language are silent: the Wernicke area, Broca area, inner talk area and inner dialogue area. Areas associated with the Thinking Faculty, Consciousness and Intellect are also silent.

- I was also able to provide scientific evidence of the four levels of samādhi: (1) samādhi with inner talk and inner dialogue, (2) samādhi without inner talk and inner dialogue, (3) Full and Clear Awareness samādhi, (4) Immobility samādhi or Tathā-Mind.

I have wished for twenty years to prove the existence of the four ultimate faculties. Only now have causal conditions been met. I feel satisfied. Now, when I teach about the ultimate faculties of the Wordless Awareness Mind, I have sufficient data to back up my teaching.

In the old days, you did not need to prove anything when you taught meditation, but now you do. Nowadays, there are many people with a scientific mind who are interested in meditation. They do not believe as readily as superstitious people. This is why you need to give proofs when you explain meditation and guide its practice.

We can "explain and execute", but, in some aspects, we also endeavor when possible to "point to the scientific evidence" of what we explain.

Question: Master, this is a joy to all of us meditation students. You have opened a new horizon for Buddhist Zen.

Answer: This is the joy of being able to prove that Buddhist Zen is an experimental spiritual science.

POSTFACE

Postface

Venerable Head Zen Master of the Sunyata Meditation Monastery sent me a copy of this book "Zen and Contemporary Knowledge – a Commentary Treatise in Question and Answer Format" with this request: "Phước Tịnh, could you please write a few words for this edition of this book". In truth, when I visited Zen Master two years before at the monastery, he had already made this request to me. At the time, I said to him "Master, please excuse me from this task". But I understood that it was a mark of his deep love and sympathy that he wanted to include a few words from his fellow practitioner. This was a way to express to the new generation the warm feelings that exist between brother practitioners of the same school. This was the reason why I felt obliged to write a few words as an appendix to this book.

We have known each other since before 1975 when we were at the Chân Không monastery, and met again at the Thường Chiếu monastery. Venerable Head Zen Master of the Sunyata School was there as one of the founding members of the Thường Chiếu monastery when it was inaugurated in the spring of 1974. Time passed, the history of our country turned a page and the tide of causal conditions ebbed and flowed. Master was sent to "study and retreat in the concentration camps of North Vietnam". I remember Thường Chiếu in those days with its meditation hall, now the floor of the guest house, and its tin roof and wooden walls. It was a far cry from its current day splendor and beauty, but it felt very warm and sweet to us. After meditation practice, we brother practitioners would lay a straw mat on the courtyard under the full moon and gather around Master and listen to him recount the many changes that occurred in the pre-1975 South Vietnamese political scene as if they were vivid pages from a book. We were full of admiration.

Master had a very broad understanding, deep thinking, and analysis covering many areas of human knowledge that he brought to his perspective on each topic together with his extensive life experience. These formed a strong foundation and brought a humanistic quality to the area of research and meditation practice that he achieves today.

Evidently, the books that Master wrote, the meditation practice that he taught students everywhere, the curriculum of his meditation classes, and the spiritual practice program and monastic life at his spiritual centers have brought great benefits to overseas Vietnamese and Westerners in many Western countries. Through its practice method and its practical interpretation of spiritual realization based on the foundations of neuroscience, a prime area of research of Western scientists, the Sunyata school has provided a valuable and useful gift to contemporary human knowledge. But its contribution is even more important through the following factors.

First, the Sunyata method is a very systematic practice method that ranges from the fundamental level suitable to people who are new to meditation to the level of those who aspire to attain intuitive wisdom and experience ultimate liberation.

Second, all practice methods of samādhi (stillness of mind), paññā (wisdom), samatha (tranquility) and anupassanā (contemplation) are very clearly explained and accompanied with techniques that facilitate their practice.

Third, Sunyata mobilizes the treasure trove of wisdom that comes with the Buddha's enlightenment and is captured in the Early Buddhism Pāli suttas to explain in detail the levels of consciousness and spiritual realization along the spiritual journey.

Last, Master has made his own body available to scientific experimentation in order to show how the state of samādhi is manifested in the human brain and nervous system.

In summary, Master's book encapsulates the three characteristics of being a serious academic work, a profound spiritual experiential testimony, and a meditation practice map for all those who thirst for a spiritual experience while living in this world.

There are books written on literature, religion, or government that are created in a restricted environment, with immature emotional reasoning or limited life experience. They may generate some temporary enthusiasm in readers but would soon fade from memory as if they never existed. There are also books written about meditation that explain the experiential spiritual path using the thinking process of the conscious mind which, with the passage of time and the maturing of human consciousness, will be progressively abandoned.

This book by Venerable Head Zen Master of the Sunyata Meditation Monastery has germinated from his very real experiential spiritual practice, then validated and interpreted through examination of, and reconciliation against, the suttas. For this reason, I do not think this book will appeal to the mass of readers. But it will certainly be a companion to the serious and prudent student, especially practitioners who want to experience true spiritual insights and step by step enter the world of immobile suchness of the true mind.

POSTFACE

As a final word, I would like to sincerely thank Venerable Head Zen Master and the Sunyata Meditation Association for showing me such warm feelings that kindle our sense of brotherhood in our days of wandering this world and living the dhamma.

At Đại Ân Sơn, Lộc Uyển Monastery
July 20th, 2014
Phước Tịnh

www.ingramcontent.com/pod-product-compliance
Lightning Source LLC
Chambersburg PA
CBHW070535010526
44118CB00012B/1139